Derek Bridges has been involved in the world of flower arranging for more than twenty years and is famous for witty, entertaining demonstrations in which he amazes audiences with his deft, apparently effortless transformation of a bunch of flowers into an arrangement of breathtaking ingenuity and beauty.

In *Derek Bridges' Flower Arranger's Bible* he reveals the secrets of his skill and experience in a book which covers every aspect of the flower arranger's art from simple displays of spring or wild flowers to arrangements of hothouse blooms for grand occasions.

The novice will find all the basic information he or she needs – from the tools of the trade and the basic principles of design to what flowers to grow or buy, what containers to choose as well as a section on drying and preserving. Derek then goes on to demonstrate a series of arrangements for all seasons and occasions – from posies for a country cottage to elaborate setpieces for a stately home, flowers for a church or cathedral, party pieces for Christmas, and how to use flowers, foliage, fruits, berries, even vegetables, in garlands, swags and collages as well as arrangements. And, finally, for the really confident, Derek offers invaluable advice on preparing for shows and competitions.

Derek Bridges is a member of the National Association of Flower Arrangement Societies (NAFAS) and has the rare distinction of demonstrating, teaching, competing and judging for them. He gives many demonstrations each year in the United Kingdom and abroad, and still likes the thrill of competing, being the first man to win the NAFAS Best of Show trophy. His wife, Pat, runs a flower arrangers' accessories shop, and together they have created the perfect flower arranger's garden, on a hillside a thousand feet above Hebden Bridge in Yorkshire.

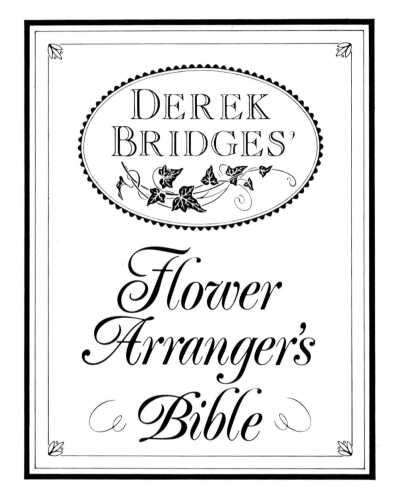

Derek Bridges'

Flower Arranger's Bible

PHOTOGRAPHY BY TREVOR RICHARDS

CENTURY PUBLISHING LONDON

To my two girls, Patricia and Sara

STOCK PHOTOGRAPHS ON PAGES 40, 41, 43, 44, AND 116
SUPPLIED BY MICHAEL BOYS SYNDICATION

PHOTOGRAPHS ON PAGES 130 AND 137
REPRODUCED BY PERMISSION OF *THE FLOWER ARRANGER*

BOOK DESIGN BY BOB HOOK
EDITED BY SUSAN FLEMING

FIRST PUBLISHED IN GREAT BRITAIN IN 1985 BY
CENTURY HUTCHINSON LTD,
BROOKMOUNT HOUSE, 62–65 CHANDOS PLACE,
COVENT GARDEN, LONDON WC2N 4NW
REPRINTED 1986

BRITISH LIBRARY CATALOGUING IN PUBLICATION DATA
BRIDGES, DEREK
THE FLOWER ARRANGER'S BIBLE.
1. FLOWER ARRANGEMENT
I. TITLE
745.92   SB449

ISBN 0-7126-0789-7

PRINTED IN GREAT BRITAIN IN 1985 BY
PURNELL & SONS (BOOK PRODUCTION) LTD, PAULTON, BRISTOL

CONTENTS

INTRODUCTION

any books have already been written on the art of flower arranging, and you may be wondering what justification there is for yet another. The reason, as far as I'm concerned, is simple. Each and every flower arranger has his or her individual creativity, imagination, way of expressing the art through the basic principles – and I wanted to share *my* ideas. Although most books undoubtedly do cover the same ground, this one is unique to me, with concepts that I like, that have worked for me, and that can be adopted, adapted and probably even improved by beginner and expert alike.

Flower arranging, although ancient, is a modern, advancing art, and these days non-professional and professional flower arrangers alike have to stay one step ahead of an increasingly enlightened public. This is another reason for the publication of my ideas. Books which appeared, say, twenty years ago, may be basically sound on various principles such as colour and shape, but other ideas will probably be out of date now: mechanics – the equipment used as a foundation for arrangements – have advanced amazingly; ideas in general have changed concerning texture, the natural flow of plant materials, the usage of less usual materials such as vegetables – and we now have a much greater choice of flowers themselves.

Flower arranging is an increasingly popular art. The principal organisation in Britain is NAFAS, the National Association of Flower Arrangement Societies. They have clubs and affiliates the length and breadth of Britain, and a membership of over 100,000. If we add to that number the people attending private, adult education and school classes, and those who just like to have fresh flowers in their homes, I reckon that some 250,000 people are arranging flowers every week in Britain alone! An international organisation, WAFA, the World Association of Flower Arrangers, was founded recently, and the member countries include Australia, Belgium, Kenya, South Africa, Cyprus, Malta and the West Indies.

And this aspect, to me, is one of the major pleasures of being involved in this art. As a full-time flower arranging demonstrator, I travel up and down Britain the entire year through to flower clubs on the NAFAS circuit. I find meeting people who share the same interests, the same love of growing and working with beautiful plant materials, is sheer joy. And when I travel abroad – to Cyprus, the West Indies and Australia this year alone – the same applies: differences do not seem to matter: the flowers speak for us.

But flower arrangers come in all types and stages. To some, who belong to clubs and attend classes and demonstrations, who compete in shows, and organise church festivals, flower arranging is a way of life. To others, flower arranging is a wonderful way of decorating their homes, and this could be a major hobby. And, of course, there are many who are beginners, who know little about the art, and who would like to know more. To all of these my book is addressed.

There will be something here

for everyone, as the book consists of a general survey of the whole field of flower arranging. In the first chapters I am perhaps talking to the less experienced. The tools of the trade are the mechanics, the necessities without which no flower arranger could operate; and containers too are vital to the look of a finished arrangement and concept. I pride myself particularly on utilising a vast array of containers both traditional and, occasionally, unusual to say the least!

The basic principles of the art are vital to an understanding of your ingredients – the plant materials – and an ability to use them in the best and most creative way. These principles – of design, colour and texture – are the foundation stones upon which a practitioner can build, using his or her imagination and talents to create an individual piece of art. They are not difficult, but take *time* to learn. By trial and error (not too much of the latter hopefully), experience will be acquired, the sense of colour developed, and the consciousness of the interest of different textures will become second nature.

These principles are most easily acquired if you can develop your own flower arranger's garden, as I have done at home, 1,000 feet above Hebden Bridge in Yorkshire. There is a very important association between horticulture and flower arranging – which is not as obvious as you might think! By growing, cultivating and handling plants from seed to maturity, throughout all the seasons of the year, you will naturally acquire a knowledge of the subtleties and differences of colours, forms and textures, and the individual beauties of individual plants. But even if you haven't a garden, a tub at the back door or a box on a window sill can still be utilised to grow what will be most useful for the flower arranger – the foliages so seldom available in florists' shops. And, perhaps the most vital part of preparation for flower arranging, I give full instructions on how to extend the life of plant materials.

Thereafter, of course, the chapters consist of arrangements and the varying ideas behind them: I cover in detail how to arrange flowers for church; how to decorate your home, whether a simple traditional cottage, a modern apartment, or a stately home, with the glories of plant materials; and I also give some ideas on how to arrange flowers for special occasions. To Christmas, the high point of the flower arranger's calendar (of mine anyway), I have given a whole chapter. In the essay on preserved plant materials, I both detail how to preserve plants – drying, glycerining etc – and how to use them in less usual decorative ways – in swags, garlands, collages and pyramids. Finally, I give some tips about preparing for shows, competitions, festivals and demonstrating!

I do hope that this book *will* be a 'bible' for you. Please do remain aware, though, that the ideas and concepts are those that have worked for me: you may have completely different tastes and aims – but then that's what flower arranging is all about, being individual! And it's worth remembering here that it's not what we know, it's what we still have to learn. I'm *still* learning after over twenty years, and I still answer promptly when asked what I'm doing in what is traditionally thought of as a woman's world: 'Enjoying every minute of it'!

CHAPTER ONE

THE TOOLS
OF THE TRADE

lower arranging is an art form first and foremost – as are painting, sculpture or needlework – and the tools of the trade are as vital for the flower arranger as the paintbrush is to the painter, the hammer to the sculptor and the needle to the embroiderer. Many of the basic tools you will already possess: the most obvious are a good pair of scissors, secateurs, and a strong, sharp knife. Other necessities, apart from the containers and the medium which will hold the flowers in the container, are floral foam tape, pinholders, florists' wires of all kinds (stub, reel and silver), cocktail sticks, skewers, pins and plasticine. If some of these seem rather remotely connected with flower arranging, it can get worse. As you become more confident, more inventive, your stock of necessities will grow. Anything, but anything – if it can do a useful job – can take its place in the flower arranger's equipment. Keep all this – your basic equipment or tools – in a plastic tool box like that illustrated on the right.

MECHANICS

Every flower arrangement should look complete, easy, graceful and effortless – never giving any hint of the backstage mechanics which have helped create such beauty. And to learn thoroughly how to deal with and use these mechanics must be virtually one of the first

tasks for a flower arranger: how to fasten a pinholder into a container, how to soak and tape down floral foam, how properly to anchor candles, fruit and other decorative items. When these basics are mastered, the flower arranger can gain confidence to become more inventive, can be assured that, whatever the idea, however unusual, he or she will be able to carry it out. Do take time to master these basic techniques.

FLORAL FOAM

One of the most important of the mechanics is floral foam, and what we did before it, I don't know. There are a great number of commercial brands on the market, with different sizes, colours, names and

One of the principal joys of being a flower arranger is that it allows one (especially me) to indulge in collecting containers of all sorts. Glass containers are particular favourites of mine, and I have recently started to collect Victorian posy vases. Although small, you can see how effective they are gathered together, one holding a simple bunch of golden lilies.

My plastic tool box with all its little divisions is probably the one single item without which I could not possibly operate. It holds all the essentials together in one place, and it goes everywhere with me – to demonstrations, shows and exhibitions. Whenever a fellow-competitor asks if someone has a pin or a hammer, the answer always comes: 'Ask Derek, he's sure to have what you want in his tool box'! The most important thing to remember, though, is to keep it tidy.

qualities, and most are good. It is a water-retaining plastic foam which is wedged into a container – or held there by plastic foam tape – and into which the flowers are arranged.

It must be soaked first. Cut or carve your foam to the shape required, then place it in a bucket of cold water. It will take about 10–15 minutes for most blocks to take up the water (one of the large blocks will absorb about 3 pints or over 1.5 litres of water). When it sinks to the water level and the bubbles stop, it is ready to be taped or wedged into its container. If the block can be wedged, no other anchorage will be needed, but both plastic and metal holders for holding down soaked floral foam are available. Floral foam sticky tape is invaluable, too, and I would not be without a reel in my tool box.

I must at this stage say that if the block is re-usable (if, say, you can turn it over and use its unholed side), but you are not going to use it straightaway, keep it in a plastic bag. If the block is allowed to dry out, it will not resoak.

Dri-foam, a generic name for a floral foam used dry, mainly for dried flower arrangements, will be discussed in Chapter Eight.

PINHOLDERS

These are still widely used, especially for simple line arrangements in low flat dishes. When fixing a pinholder onto the base of your container there are one or two points that must be mentioned. Firstly make sure that the container and pinholder are clean and dry. Roll out a long sausage shape of plasticine or other adhesive clay to about $\frac{1}{4}$ inch (6 mm) thick, and place around the base edge of the pinholder so that you have a complete circle. Press the clay or plasticine side of the pinholder onto the container base, pushing down and spreading out the sausage shape. Turn the pinholder at the same time as you press, and the pinholder should adhere to the container. You are now ready to start the arrangement.

WIRE NETTING

This is still used by many flower arrangers, and in very large arrangements is useful placed over the top of floral foam like a hairnet to give extra support. It is available from your local hardware shop. Always buy the larger mesh: the 2-inch (5-cm) size is best. When using wire netting on its own, once the piece has been cut (some metal cutters in your tool box!), ease it into a ball shape, remembering to keep it fairly loose. If you shape the ball too tightly, you will find it difficult to get your required number of stems through into the water. The advantages of using wire netting are that it will support very large stems of plant material, and it will last much longer (being galvanised) than foam which you will have to replace frequently.

CONTAINERS, BASES AND ACCESSORIES

A vital part of basic equipment is the container. It's rather difficult to know where to start, as it's such a huge subject, but, fundamentally, if it holds water, it will take an arrangement. In the past, flower containers were known as 'vases', but not many of these are used by flower arrangers now except for giving the flowers a drink before arranging them in the latest container find. Many containers will be found in flower shops and flower accessory departments, but you will find inventiveness far more fun and far more rewarding. That gravy boat with a chip in the rim: it's not too good now for the table holding gravy, but for the table holding flowers and foliage . . . now where's the chip? You will find that you cannot resist going into the local junk shop, flea market and bring-and-buy sale. You'll get some funny looks too. As you gaze at the lidless teapot, they'll think you will be using it for tea despite there being no lid, but your imagination will be running riot: a drip of ivy down by the handle, blossom and spring flowers cascading from the top – I'll have it, yours for 20 pence! See what I mean? It's all a matter of training the eye.

Don't forget either that if what you have in your hand is highly patterned and thus, you think, not suitable, don't put it down: look at the shape, it can always change colour. Spray paints are a godsend to the flower arranger. You can use car spray paints but these tend to be over-glossy; a more matt or egg-shell finish will be better. Matt black is of course obvious and I use many black containers, but you can also get earthy colours, the dull greens and browns which are nature's colours, and they will be ideal for many types and styles of arrangements. White can be useful too, but I use it only for white and green arrangements or very pale colourings: with deeper colourings, a white container seems to dominate.

BASKETRY

Basket-making must be one of the oldest handicrafts, although birds probably beat us to the technique – just think of a nest. Thousands of years ago people made baskets sim-ply for holding and gathering their grains and foods. I have in my basketry collection some modern African baskets that have been made in exactly the same way as they were when time began, and which are still used in Africa for storing foodstuffs. In the European Middle Ages, baskets were hung on doors at spring festival time, filled with fresh flowers. Commoners and royals alike in Merrie England collected flowers and blossoms in baskets; green branches from the country adorned the doors of houses in the towns; and baskets of flowers were brought – like a breath of springtime – into the houses. With all these historical associations between basketry and flowers, no wonder the combination is still so popular.

Baskets are made of natural and beautiful materials – of bamboo, rattan, straw, reeds, willow and twigs – and thus flowers have a natural affinity with them. Basketry containers can range from delicate Italian straw to rustic crude twig shapes, and on the whole they do tend to have an informal effect. They can be used at all seasons of the year: a simple basket of the first spring flowers, for instance, or a rougher basket with the glories of dried grasses, autumn berries and fruits.

When using a basketry container, don't forget that it ought to be *seen*, and it ought in many cases to be lined first with something which fits and which can hold water – a tin, a tray or something similar, paint-sprayed a dull colour if necessary to prevent rust, and so that the colour melts into the shadows of the arrangement. Basketry can be a wonderful accessory too – fans, platters, trays, stands etc. Look at the photograph on page 12

Everyone who has seen me demonstrating knows that I have a passion for basketry and baskets. I have collected over 170 pieces now, from here, there and everywhere, and you can see just how varied a collection it is. If I am still arranging flowers thirty years from now, I shall still be collecting baskets, it's such a never-ending source of supply.

In the glorious setting of Warwick Arts, London, on a rosewood table, I have utilised some shells as an integral part of a strikingly sparse arrangement. I nailed a piece of driftwood onto a slice of wood, and then affixed three pearl shells onto convenient clefts. I taped small blocks of floral foam into the two main shells, leaving the third empty as a feature. The flowers are Singapore (dendrobium) orchids and the foliage is croton.

of my own collection of basketry which demonstrates just how many shapes, sizes and types of basketry can be useful to the flower arranger.

TREASURES OF THE SEA SHORE

Everyone seems to be drawn to the sea, even if only to paddle, but the flower arranger is drawn there because of what he or she might find. Driftwood or shells can form part of a hundred compositions. The beauty of a seashell, the shape and strength of a piece of sea-sculpted driftwood, can all set the mind ticking over. Many shells make containers themselves, others are used as accessories, and you can see from the photographs opposite and on page 13 how shells can be used beautifully in arrangements as well as just grouped together as a fascinating feature, a combination of shapes, colours and textures. You can buy many beautiful shells now in gift shops, but if you are lucky enough to travel to hot climates, you will of course go beach-combing. I have strolled for hours on African beaches and have collected some wonderful shells.

If worried about the smell (and often rightly so), the best thing to do is to wash the collected shells well, let them dry, and then put them into a plastic bag. Tie up the top securely, and by the time you get home and open the bag, the smell will make you stagger! Put the shells into a bucket of paraffin for about a week. Not only will it get rid of the smell but it also cleans them. Dry off and polish with a cloth, and all the delicate colours of the shell will be revealed.

You can also use shell-*shaped* containers and 'sea' ideas to create arrangements that will be equally successful. Look at the arrange-

I love to collect shells –
it's not just children
who do it, but flower
arrangers as well –
and here you can see
how effective they are
as a collection,
grouped together on a
shelf in my downstairs
loo. Their shapes are
interesting, the colours
are subtle and, by the
flower arranger, they
can be used either as
containers or
accessories.

Still continuing with my treasures from the sea theme, in this arrangement I used a large ceramic shell-shaped container, originally a shallow hand-basin from Spain. It is a lovely creamy colour, resting on a deep coral base. The plant material I chose does, I think, conjure up the feel of the sea. The tall curling lines are dried banana stem to which I attached pieces of sea fan coral. The flowers were more difficult – I wanted something that looked as if it might have come from the depths – and I chose coral-coloured anthuriums, the flamingo flower. The foliage, reminiscent of underwater plants, is bergenia. The mechanics of the arrangement were covered with deep coral-coloured pieces of fungus and, placed on a glass table in a bathroom, the arrangement should feel very much at home!

ment opposite, which uses a ceramic container shaped like a shell. The one difficulty of treasures-of-the-sea ideas is finding flowers and foliage that look as if they are of underwater origin – but a little thought and inventiveness, the trademarks of flower arrangers, will eventually bear fruit.

Driftwood, sculpted by the sea into fascinating shapes, is a wonderful source of inspiration, and in some cases doesn't need any other plant material. I have some pieces set up in my garden that Henry Moore would be quite happy with! Finding a piece of driftwood bleached silver by the sun, sometimes with rich rust-brown colours running through it, makes it a positive pleasure to go beachcombing. It can be easy, though, to get carried away with beach finds (you've got to get them home first,

Whenever beachcombing, keep your eyes open for interesting pieces of driftwood. The sea sculpts wood into such fascinating shapes, many of which are ideal 'containers' for the flower arranger. The piece here is so primitive looking that it needs little else apart from five proteas (from South Africa) and hosta foliage. The flowers and foliage are threaded into the crevices of the wood and wedged. I have also used the same piece of wood in a vertical position, fixed into another piece of wood as a base. Even using the same flowers and foliage, it creates a quite different picture and combination of shapes and textures.

remember), and you may at first put too many together in an arrangement. Try to decide which of the materials to combine and always avoid too much clutter. In most cases when you have decided on the basics, it might only need just a little plant material; look at the photograph on page 17 which uses only a few flowers and a minimum of foliage, allowing the natural and beautiful form of the driftwood to shine forth. The piece of breakwater, too, opposite, is used as a wonderful container for some striking flowers and foliage.

METAL

Metal containers and accessories are great favourites with flower arrangers, as they offer such stimulating possibilities. Just think of the number of household articles that have been made over the centuries from the various metals, most of which can be used in some way by the flower arranger. Everyone at one time wanted to possess a brass candlestick or copper tea urn, but metal containers are infinitely more varied than that: pots, kettles, jugs, bowls, trays, plates and figurines. Look at your own collection of metal objects for their flower-arranging possibilities, and scour junk shops for objects which may be just what you need. Super containers can be bought abroad, haggled over in some Eastern souk, perhaps.

Any metal is suitable for the flower arranger, and almost any shape: the copper kettle to hold an arrangement, the brass tray to act as a base or background accessory, or even the gold candlestick topped with a glory of toning flowers and foliages. Always use the colour and gleam of your metal to give you your theme. A silver container doesn't necessarily have to hold the perhaps traditional pink roses or sweet peas – although lovely and very feminine. Why not use orange, red or even deep purple flowers? A spray of grey foliage will relate well, the shiny metal against the dull matt surface of the leaves. Silver is sophisticated, though, so match your flowers, arrangement and setting to that sophistication. Pewter, on the other hand, an alloy of tin with antimony, copper or (usually) lead, is more down to earth, rustic and 'folksy' – relating of course to its more generally domestic use, prior to mass-produced earthenware. But, whatever you do, do not let yourself be stereotyped: try something different, out of the ordinary – it may be stunning.

Pewter and spelter – a related metal, but with the addition of zinc – are favourites of mine, and I have a good collection of containers in both. I have many pewter and Britannia metal coffee and tea pots, and a much prized collection of spelter ewers (see page 20) which I use a lot in my arrangements. The ewer shape is very effective indeed, as a container or as an accessory, and you can also see it classically beautiful in alabaster in the photograph on page 21, and in that of the magnificent gilded table in the Christmas chapter.

Spelter, a soft metal, is often covered with another surface in an attempt to make it more sophisticated. I prefer it in its original colour, but if you find a spelter figure, say, with a painted surface and it's in good condition, leave it. If not, some work with brown shoe polish gives a super effect after a while. Whatever happens, never use spray paints on spelter pieces – any value will be taken away, both

Still using wood sculpted by the sea, this is a tall piece of breakwater standing on a slate base. Although potentially unpromising, it makes a magnificent container for flowers and foliage. The yellow gladioli give height and colour, with lilies ('Connecticut King') in the centre; the dark green is hosta, and the two main feature foliages are ananas or pineapple plants.

financial and visual. And if you find a spelter piece that has been spray-painted, a paint stripper will clean it up, before you get to work with that shoe polish.

Pedestal containers, those on stems, to give height, are usually made of metal. They can be mass-produced from the florists' suppliers, or individual works of art. See examples of pedestal arrangements in Chapter Four.

Metal containers for flower arrangers come in all shapes and sizes, but my particular favourites are ewers, and I use them often in arrangements because the shape is so good, either as accessories, or with an arrangement in the top. This is part of my own collection, and it shows what a variety is available. Those illustrated are mainly made of spelter, although some have porcelain centre bowls which add another dimension.

Two ewers in alabaster look wonderfully classical in a niche in my sitting room. Simple and elegant with only a splash of muted colour from the artificial grapes, they would look magnificent as part of, or holding, an arrangement.

Items of coloured glass, simple, elegant and cool, look wonderful grouped together in this way. All, individually, could act as containers, but combined thus – their shapes and colours offsetting and blending with each other – against the backdrop of leaves outside, they create a beautiful stained-glass window effect.

GLASS

Glass must never be forgotten, and containers made from this medium have long been favourites with the flower arranger. Bowls, goblets and plates of great beauty and colour: all are transparent and translucent, sparkling and lustrous. At one time, cut-glass vases were *the* thing into which to put flowers, but they're not quite suitable for to-day's flower arranger. Lovely and less usual forms in delicate and rich colours are the types of glass containers and accessories that the modern arranger finds most pleasing to use. Italy, of course, has always produced lovely pieces, as has Sweden, with its clean, understated lines. (Swedish glass is much heavier than Italian glass.) If clear glass is what you fancy, Holland is now producing some good pieces. Also look out on holiday for rough-made glass – usually locally produced – that may be primitive, but can have a natural beauty and interest. One of the most interesting things about these rough pieces is that they are all hand-made, so no two pieces can be the same.

Glass has interested me for many years and in fact I collect old drinking glasses – I know I like what goes into them – but of course these are not ideal for flower arranging. I have also started to collect Victorian posy vases, and you can see from the photograph on page 8 just how effective they are grouped together. But it's coloured glass that I find most exciting in arrangements: look at my blue glass grouped together in a window, at its shapes and colours; there are pieces from Malta, from Spain and Sweden, side by side with an old piece of Bristol Blue – with the surprising addition of two glass bricks from the local builders' merchants! Just think what the addition of flowers and foliages could create.

CERAMICS

Ceramic containers – those products of earth and fire, which have been made since man first walked the earth – are held in high regard by all flower arrangers, whether simple rough pots, unglazed earthenware or beautiful fine china. There are four main groups of ceramics – earthenware, china, stoneware and porcelain – and the differences are based on the degrees of heat at which pieces are fired: porcelain is subjected to the highest heat, unglazed earthenware to the lowest. Early man developed claypot making by moulding clay over woven baskets then letting it dry, or by rolling wet clay into long ropes and coiling them into shapes, building up a pot row upon row. Modern potters generally work in two ways, either casting in or on moulds or by throwing on a wheel, and there are many potters now producing some very beautiful – and very expensive – pieces. This is one of the reasons why, in my early days of flower arranging, I went to an evening class to learn how to make my own containers. I still have some of these, and they are among my most prized possessions.

As with metal containers, use your ceramics in designs and arrangements suited to the piece: sophistication with the cool lines of the best porcelain, simpler and more homely with a hand-thrown pot, like that in the photograph on page 24. The simplicity of the pot is echoed by the sparse and striking use of the stripped ivy and the flowers and foliage. And don't forget that ceramics too, like glass, can

A hand-thrown ceramic pot is an ideal container for the simplest of arrangements, and the two wicker fans act as a complementary base. The colours are echoed by the high swirling line of stripped ivy – creating a wonderful rhythm. A few scarlet anthuriums (flamingo flowers) and leaves of arum (Italicum) are the natural plant materials.

As with glass, ceramic containers can be grouped together. These two, sitting on top of a hi-fi speaker, have wonderfully natural colours and the lilies ('Enchantment') pick up the slip colours of the containers. The simple sweeping line is created by berried branches of cornus. The other foliage is helleborus.

be grouped together as on page 25. Together the two containers and their related plant material contents make for a strong but simple line.

FIGURINES

Regardless of material or size, figurines have always been sought after by flower arrangers. Whether made of metal, wood, stone, clay or ivory, whether they represent human or animal shapes, when incorporated into an arrangement, figurines can look very exciting and interesting. The term figurine to most people means a small figure or statuette, but even life-sized pieces can be used. Figurines are especially popular with flower arrangers who compete in flower shows, but you can have great fun utilising them at home as well.

The important thing to remember is scale – an important element in *all* arrangements. When figurines are involved in a composition, our eyes seem to be even more discerning, more critical, and we will not be happy with the finished effect if the figurine is out of scale. It should be neither too small, when it may be lost completely amongst the greenery, nor should it be too large – the plant material must predominate. But there is a nice happy medium. Indeed, some flower arrangers feel that figurines should not be used in arrangements, that they should only be displayed separately. Both sides have a point, but I believe figurines bring a challenging element to the arrangement and afford special opportunities to use your imagination.

For figurines can be used to stimulate, and to tell a story, and I enjoy using them. They must be selected with discrimination, though, and used with thought. It is the stereotyped figurines of which you can tire, so it's a never-ending search for something different. A ceramic or metal figure or a hand-carved one-off wooden model could be a prized possession. If you plan to include it in a composition, make an effort to discover just what the figure represents. Every good piece of art has something to say. Look at the use I have made of two of my figurines on the next few pages. The material used with the wooden African statuette is reminiscent of the sandy, hot African savannah from which she must surely come; and the boldness of the flowers, as well as their colour, echoes the martial theme of the gilded warrior.

If you want to use mass-produced figurines, do make sure they are of good quality. Some are hand-painted in delicate colours and have a container bowl in the top, in which the arrangement can be made. But whichever you use – mass-produced or individual pieces of art – I find it best to have figures on display for a short while only, and then to put them out of sight. When you bring them out again, they will take on a new meaning and look totally different from the last time they were used.

BASES AND LIFTS

Bases underneath a container are not essential, but in many cases can improve the setting. I think a base is like an island for the arrangement to live on, a frame for the floral picture you have painted – it shows off the arrangement. Of course, if you are going to use a base, it must be in harmony with the container and the arrangement. You would not, for example, put a lovely china figurine onto a rough hessian-

This photograph is a prime example of how figurines can be used in arrangements. The beautiful slim figure of a girl – hand-carved in Africa – seemed to need complementary colours and materials, as well as feel. I thought the dried exotic material was just right – she would not have been happy with daffodils or tulips from the northern hemisphere! From a small piece of styrofoam behind her, the height is carried by clipped palmetto sprays, and weight is brought down to the base with curled giant bean pods, African seed heads, and one large dried artichoke. The wood slice base just finishes off the design.

covered base; neither would you put a piece of driftwood onto velvet. So, as well as collecting containers and figurines, you could also start collecting bases: simple rush place mats are a good way to start, followed by slices of log, pieces of slate and stone.

Bases can also be used on their own with no actual container visible. In this case you will have a small container to hold your floral foam or pinholder, which you should paint if necessary. It could have been an empty sardine tin or potted meat holder, but it will still hold an arrangement. Covered cake boards also make very useful bases. I am not too keen on those bases covered with fabric that has been seamed and then elastic run through. Although one base can have many covers, which is useful, they are never completely smooth-looking.

I prefer to make my own bases. I cut fibreboard to the shape required – oblong, square, round etc – and then cut the chosen fabric to fit, but slightly larger than the board. Apply quick-drying glue around the side edges of the board and stretch, press and pull the fabric so that it adheres to the glued sides of the board. Push straight dressmakers' pins into the fibrous board edges through the material at 3-inch (7.5-cm) intervals to hold it firm. Trim the material well, and don't bother to take out the pins when the glue has dried. Cover the pinheads and the cut edges of the material with some glued-on matching or contrasting braid which gives a good finish. This makes a good neat base, and a major advantage is that because there is no surplus material or gathers underneath, it will sit flat on the furniture.

Lifts or plinths are used to give height to a container or figurine. These are as simple to devise as the bases and can be covered in the same materials. A coffee tin or similar straight-sided box shape covered in the same fabric as the base can make all the difference to a finished design. A figurine, for instance, could be dwarfed by the plant material, but raising it up a few inches on a covered lift can make it more important within the design. And see also page 73 for an unusual lift – a column made of grey plastic fall pipe!

Just as with containers, look out for things that will act as lifts – blocks of marble or wood to go under an arrangement container to give height. A few years ago I found an old biscuit tin which was square in shape, with the sides painted to look like marble: it goes wonderfully with a green urn that I use a lot. Look out too for those delightful oriental scroll bases which are dark, good-looking and will prove a welcome addition to your collection.

I have outlined the basic tools, mechanics and main groups of containers, but in all areas, there will be many more things you will find you acquire, need and cannot work without. Once you start it will never stop. No guests in the spare room – it's been taken over – or will you need another shed in the garden? I've mentioned shells and driftwood as containers and accessories, but what about coral, stones and coloured sands . . . Basketry I covered in great detail but what about lined wooden containers – tea caddies, boxes etc. Don't forget my main criterion concerning containers: if it holds water, it can hold a flower arrangement.

In complete contrast to the African figurine and its subtle muted feel, this gilded warrior figure needed a bold approach. One of a set of three, he is made from scrap metal, and his shield is of welded bolts. To echo this, I used gilded lotus seed pods which spray out from the foot of the arrangement – what I call togetherness! I used red, a man's colour, for the flowers – gladioli, carnations and anthuriums (flamingo flowers) and various varieties of fern for the foliage outline.

CHAPTER TWO

THE PRINCIPLES OF FLOWER ARRANGING

lower arranging is such a personal art that there really should be no rules. There are some basic guidelines, though, which you should be aware of before you start, and which should always be at the back of your mind. The flowers and foliages you use in any arrangement must first be well conditioned (see the next chapter), and if possible the flowers should be in various stages of development for interest – buds, half open, and full blooms. Never cut your flowers or foliages to the same length, and indeed never cut them at all (except when picking of course) until you are actually placing them in the arrangement, when you can *see* what length of stem you require. You want to have an in-and-out appearance to your arrangement, with recessed flowers and foliages to give a three-dimensional, not flat, appearance. Group flowers in sweeps not blocks, and of course always work on an arrangement at the angle or angles from which it will be seen.

Finally, and most importantly, allow your plant material to 'dictate' to you, not the other way round, how it should fall or lie within the arrangement. If you can,

study foliage before you cut, for instance, to determine its line and shape, to see if it will be what you require. You will not want everything straight and poker-like, and it would be a shame to cut and not use it. (A bit difficult if you have stopped the car, having seen something interesting or growing wild, and want to take it home to try out.) Plant materials are always beautiful in their natural state, and it's that natural beauty that you wish to recreate in your arrangements.

DESIGN

Over the centuries people have always enjoyed putting flowers and branches into pots, but I think we may have simply enjoyed the beauty of the plant materials themselves rather than considered the design. There are still many people who think that flowers look best 'popped into a pot', that flower arrangers spoil the plant materials by being over-contrived. I, of course, disagree. Mother Nature certainly started it all off, but I think we just slightly adapt and improve. Design is a working plan, the art of making decorative patterns and, according to one dictionary definition – 'crafty scheming'. (I wonder if this definition should

Many people find green an uninteresting colour, but how can you be a flower arranger and not like green! One of my favourite borders in my own garden is all green, from the darkest to the palest, and I defy anyone not to see the wonderful variety of colours as exhibited in this photograph. Wood slices propped on a wooden base hold my best-loved greens – cornus, hosta, euphorbia and astrantia (variegata).

be applied to competitive flower arrangers!) Design, whether simple or elaborate, *must* be part of the flower arranger's basic starting points.

TRADITIONAL ARRANGEMENTS

These are the most commonly seen designs, as we seem to like the profuse arrangements of flowers and foliage, and they go so well in most of our homes. Traditional designs are also known as 'massed arrangements', and this certainly applied a few years ago when many arrangements seemed to have a mass of everything: if you've got it, put it in! As the use of containers changed, and the varieties of mechanics improved and progressed, traditional arrangements became more stylised and more thought out; arrangers seem now, thankfully, to study much more the flow of a piece of foliage or spray of berries, thus getting the best from every piece of plant material.

From the photographs and captions opposite and on page 34, you will understand in much more detail the principles and working stages of a traditional or massed arrangement. The vertical lines – the spine of the arrangement – are created first, placed towards the back of the soaked floral foam securely wedged in the container. The side lines, using the natural sweep of the plant material, are the next placements into the side of the floral foam. Now that these basics are accomplished, the area which you have to 'fill' with flowers and foliage is apparent. I would always strengthen the foliage at this stage, remembering to recess, using different colours and textures (see later in this chapter for more details). The flowers can then be placed to your design, using col-

ours and shapes to highlight, complement and strengthen the original flowing lines. The focal-point flowers should always be the last placements, their glories bringing together all the elements of your design. Although superficially a 'massed' arrangement, I'm sure you will agree that the lines in the arrangement are still clear and that every flower can be seen, unlike many massed arrangements of the past.

LINE ARRANGEMENTS

This term is normally applied to a sparse vertical or upright arrangement, which contains very little plant material. Line is a directional path that each object of the composition traces through space. It can be the length from top to bottom of a flower stalk and, as in the traditional arrangement, it's the strong vertical line that is all-important. This vertical line could be created by three tall bulrushes accompanying five blue irises, or by a sweeping branch of shrub or indeed tree. The photograph on page 37 shows a vertical line created by a well-trimmed branch of silver birch which gently sweeps upwards.

People often believe that these tall forceful arrangements would only be suitable for the modern home. In my old house, I do many similar arrangements, and I don't think they look out of place at all. But the containers are all-important for these arrangements, and they must be chosen carefully. Something simple in style or design is what to look out for, as too much decoration can cause confusion. There are many suitable commercial containers on the market, and you should be able to find more individual pieces. If you cannot find what you want, once again I urge you to do as I did and join the local pottery class. In fact the container in the picture is one that I made, and although simple and straightforward, has proved very useful over the years.

HORIZONTAL ARRANGEMENTS

As height is the important element in a line or vertical arrangement, it is the width that is the principal feature of a horizontal design. All the basic principles apply – apart from that strong vertical line – and this style of arrangement is most useful as a dining-table arrangement where it is so important to keep the height line fairly low – you want your facing guests to be able to see and talk to each other! Horizontal arrangements can also be used on side tables and in churches (see pages 66, 80 and 85 for some pictorial examples).

ALL-ROUND ARRANGEMENTS

The traditional and line arrangements already mentioned and illus-

These step-by-step pictures of a traditional arrangement will illustrate far more clearly than words the basic principles of this type of flower arranging, and of how I work on an arrangement.

1. *Always start with the outline of the arrangement, to get the height and width; the primary placement is usually a vertical. This is the arrangement's strongest line – the backbone or spine. Vigorous and upward reaching, these sprays of bottlebrush and eucalyptus suggest firmness and force. Branches of euonymus and ruscus create the flowing side lines. These too are important, setting the width of the arrangement.*

3. *Flowers should be chosen to follow the same line of the foliage. The first to go into the arrangement are sprays of commercially produced lilac (syringa), placed vertically and gradually flowing to the sides. These are followed by sprays of mimosa. (A difficult blossom, as it tends to dry up so quickly inside heated houses. Do try to buy it when young.)*

2. *Once the vertical and horizontal outlines have been established, you can see the area that the arrangement is to fill. The foliage is now strengthened with vertical, horizontal and recessed foliage: elaeagnus to the outside for lightness; camellia foliage and young spikes of euphorbia (wulfenii) towards the centre; and, to add a further touch of lightness, a forward flowing spray of ivy (hedera canariensis).*

4. *As the arrangement is now beginning to take on its desired effect, the principal flowers can start to be included. I have used blue Dutch irises for shape to the right and back, and their yellow 'noses' are picked up and complemented by the yellow of the daffodils ('Fortune').*

To complete the step-by-step arrangement, I placed small tulips to echo the yellow theme, and then created the focal point of the whole composition with sprays of yellow lilies ('Connecticut King').

trated are what are known as facing arrangements. They are designed to be seen from limited angles only, not all-round, and should of course be sited where the back of the arrangement and the mechanics cannot be seen. Horizontal arrangements placed on a side table can be a facing arrangement as well, but obviously many arrangements will be seen from all sides, and must therefore be designed thus. Prime examples of all-round arrangements are those on a dining table (horizontal), or those on a central table in a hall, for example. Obviously all general design principles still apply, but vertical stems, if used, should be placed in the *middle* of the soaked floral foam in the container, instead of at the back, and the flowing horizontal stems should radiate out from it. So that you don't get a 'square' appearance, set horizontal lines as a five-pointed star, and build up from that basis. The most important thing to remember is to work the arrangement all the way round all the time. Do not complete one side and then try to copy it on the other, as it just will not work. Too much plant material will be used on the first side, and the second could look lean.

MINIATURE ARRANGEMENTS

Although I rarely do miniature arrangements (they're rather pointless for demonstration purposes!), they are delightful, and I gather that once you get hooked you're really hooked. Go to any flower show with a miniature competing class, and you will find one of the largest crowds. The formal NAFAS schedule defines miniatures as an exhibit of no more than 4 inches (10 cm) overall. The workmanship in the miniature class has to be of the highest, as the flowers, leaves and the containers – a thimble, shell or top of a perfume bottle – have to be of the correct scale. Patience is the keynote when dealing with such delicate arrangements, and a better choice for the beginner would probably be the petite arrangement. This is more than 4 inches (10 cm) but less than 9 inches (22.5 cm) overall, and there will be a greater availability of suitable plant materials. This size of arrangement would be good for a bathroom shelf or bedside table, and there will be many more containers that are right in scale and harmony – small boxes and baskets, small china and glass containers.

OTHER ARRANGEMENTS

The following styles are not represented in this book, but should just be mentioned. A *crescent arrangement* should have the clean-cut line of a new moon, and the best arrangements are on stemmed containers, a candlestick, for instance. The correct flowing lines of plant materials are needed to create that crescent shape, so it's primarily a matter of looking on the tree or shrub to see the shape. *Hogarth curve arrangements*, named after the English artist William Hogarth, are sometimes referred to as 'S' designs. As with crescent arrangements, a lifted container is best.

Two other styles of flower arranging are abstract and Ikebana. Mentioned only, because abstract I don't do, and Ikebana I am not qualified to write about.

COLOUR

Colour, to the flower-arranger, is the most beautiful aspect of the art – it is the first thing that catches the eye, the colour of a flower, a leaf, a piece of fruit. In fashion, home decor, make-up and many other disciplines apart from flower-arranging, colour is used to attract, to complement, to startle, to please. Colours, like most things, though, are personal: you may like red, someone else may hate it; you may perceive a certain red, but how can you be sure that all have that same perception as you? Look at any colour wheel, and study the six colours of the spectrum – red, orange, yellow, green, blue and violet. These are the primary colours, but it's their shades and tints that are of prime interest to the flower arranger. There are also neutral colours – black, white and grey.

A true awareness and a skilled use of colours comes, as does a fashion colour sense, with practice and experience. The more you look at and handle plant materials and think carefully about the subject, the more confident your judgements will be. An inexperienced flower-arranger will choose colours with abandon because of their eye-catching qualities, but with experience and time, attitudes will change. Colours discreetly combined in an arrangement with subtle harmonies, are much more satisfying.

Use Mother Nature herself as a guide to colour combinations. Look at a flower in detail. It won't be just one colour, but a harmonious meld of many. Look into its centre, at its foliage, even on its back, and you will begin to appreciate these harmonies. Use this heightened awareness of colour sense when planting out your flower arranger's garden border, tub or window-box. What looks good combined in the garden will also look good arranged in your home. The garden and the arrangement go hand in hand, and even the simplest combination of greens only, as in the photograph on page 30, shows the harmony of a garden border recreated in something pleasing for home decoration.

To heighten your colour awareness even further, study house-paint colour charts, shade cards of artists' colours, knitting wools and cottons, and scraps of wallpaper and fabric. Choose your container colours carefully: neutral colours will probably be best as anything too vivid confuses and distracts. And choose your arrangement colours to complement your proposed setting, to enhance the room decoration in general, and the immediate background in particular. The finished arrangement must look *right* in its setting, and it must have a personality. This can also be achieved by colours, and I associate colours with specific states of mind, etc: yellow with sunshine and cheerfulness; red, a masculine colour, with danger, excitement and richness; blue with cleanliness, sea and sky; orange with earthiness and warmth; green with woodlands and freshness; violet with richness and luxury!

TEXTURE

All surfaces have a definite textural quality. Often this quality is more easily perceived through touch rather than sight because of the make-up of the surface – smooth, rough, hairy or prickly. Texture is just as important as colour in a flower arrangement in order to obtain textural unity or contrasts.

In flower arrangements, too many textures of the same type do not create interest, so you should aim for as much contrast as possible. Imagine a gnarled piece of driftwood holding a spray of camellias: the rough wood, shiny foliage and delicate flowers will create three wonderful texture contrasts in one group. But they must also be the *right* textures.

At Christmas many arrangements are spoiled by too much glitter or too much gloss. Sprays of already glossy leaves need, say, the contrast of some velvet ribbon bows or glass baubles, so that, again, different textures make up the whole. If some leaf sprays or flowers already have glitter, don't sprinkle more glitter on other surfaces that are plain.

As with colour, collect wallpaper and fabric samples, skeins of cottons and wools, things from nature, so that your texture sense can be fully awakened.

This simple arrangement – on a dish I made many years ago in a pottery class – is an example of a line arrangement. As in the traditional arrangement, the strong vertical line is all-important, here created by a well-trimmed, upwards pointing branch of silver birch. After it was firmly placed on a heavy pinholder, I placed some stones in and around the pinholder, both to create interest and to hide the pinholder. Daffodils used in a natural group with their own foliage were placed onto the pinholder spikes. And, to complete the arrangement, I used one of my favourite foliages, dark green and veined arum (italicum 'Pictum').

CHAPTER THREE

GROWING AND CONDITIONING FOR FLOWER ARRANGING

lthough growing for flower arranging isn't an *absolute* necessity – as is conditioning – it does help. Flower arrangers in general grow – or should grow – the sort of things that cannot be bought: cut flowers are always available from the local flower shop, but you try and buy some interesting foliage – no chance. The answer is to grow the foliages, blossoms and berries to be used fresh and dried or preserved – all so vital to creative arrangements – in your own garden.

And conditioning, the preparing of flowers and foliage so that they will last longer in your arrangements, is the most important thing of all.

THE FLOWER ARRANGER'S GARDEN

Flower arrangers' gardens – like flower arrangers themselves – come in all shapes and sizes, from a couple of tubs by the back door to as many acres as can be comfortably managed. And in those gardens, of whatever size, many plants useful – if not vital – to successful arrangements, can be grown. I have my own favourites, many of which I grow fairly successfully at home, despite the fact that the garden is 1,000 feet (300 metres) above sea level, high in the Pennines, with a view over to Lancashire on one side, and the start of the Wuthering Heights moors on the other. The soil is peat-based, although I also use an extra six bales of peat a year. I now have a very good loamy consistency which is wonderful for most flower arrangers' gardens.

But my favourites – a selected number of which I have chosen to write about in the next few pages – will probably not be yours, nor will my choices necessarily be suitable for your climatic conditions – the south coast of England, western Ireland or the north of Scotland, say – nor for your soil. Have a look at my suggested plants, read good books on gardening, study seedsmen's catalogues, and find out what plants will grow well in your particular garden. Visit your local garden centre to view the plants that they are growing with success; don't buy straightaway, but go in spring, summer and autumn to see what you will be getting for your money (there's no point in going in winter, when many shrubs will be without their leaves).

Another major consideration is the size of your garden. Town

One of the principal joys of being a flower arranger is the buying and choosing of flowers. When preparing for the arrangement illustrated on page 80, I went to Covent Garden market (now at Nine Elms). Not everyone has the opportunity to buy at such a large and wonderful flower market, where there are floral surprises from around the world, and you cam see from the grin on my face that I'm in paradise! I have an armful of glories and I'm surrounded by colourful beauty – molucella, proteas, agapanthus, orchids and Sterling Silver roses.

A typical cottage garden with a colourful profusion of old-fashioned roses, geraniums, alchemilla (mollis), buddleia, and a seat for relaxation.

arranger to forget about colour and to go for foliage every time.

In a larger space a larger selection of plants can of course be built up. Again go for shapes – some tall plants, some bushy plants, some spreading plants, some blossom trees – and with more space available, touches of colour can happily be included. I love the cottage gardens with their hedges, borders, walls, paths, trees, and a general feeling of rich, natural and random luxuriance. Look at the photographs left and opposite to see the sort of plants, and the feeling, of both town and cottage gardens.

PLANTS TO GROW IN TUBS

The following plants all have foliage that can be picked at any time of the year, and thus are invaluable to the flower arranger with limited growing space. The larger the pot the better, of course, and you should try to choose something tall, something bushy, and something that flows.

Hedera (*canariensis* 'Variegata'), Canary Island ivy, has leaves which are dark green in the centre, which shades through silver-grey to a white border. It thrives in both sun and shade, and can be grown up trellises.

Bergenia (*purpurascens* 'Bellawley') has glossy, mid-green large leathery leaves, and is in general larger than other bergenias. Fuchsia-red flowers are produced on long stems above the foliage in April and May.

Mahonia (*japonica*) is a wonderful shrub for the limited-space garden of a flower arranger. It has dark lustrous leaves, sprays of lemon-yellow flowers in winter, and green berries in spring which ripen in summer to deep purple.

Skimmia (*japonica*) is a

gardens are usually small, often with fairly thin soil, an excess of water-leaching walls, and uneven light and shade from those same surrounding walls. The plants, whether to grow in tubs or in the actual ground, must be chosen carefully, and must be in scale with their surroundings (just as in arrangements); it's no use planting a magnificent foliage and blossom tree if it will soon grow and overshadow everything else in the garden. Try to concentrate on different shapes, textures and heights, on plants that will be useful throughout the year – evergreens, for instance – and don't take up valuable space without a return. Use any walls fruitfully, with climbing plants, and if space is severely limited, I would always advise the town-dwelling flower medium-sized shrub with pale evergreen leaves. It bears creamy white clusters of flowers in April/May, followed by red berries which ripen in August. (If you want berries, borne by the female plant, you will have to grow a male plant as well.)

Viburnum (*tinus*) is another evergreen shrub with large leaves that are mid to deep green. It has white, pink-budded flowers at the end of shoots from November to May. Many also bear berries.

Elaeagnus (*pungens*) is one of the most brilliant of winter shrubs, with glossy oval leaves splashed in the centre with bright yellow, and creamy white underneath. Silvery flowers appear in October/November, sometimes followed by red or orange berries.

OTHER USEFUL SHRUBS AND TREES

Shrubs and trees that produce blossom, or good branches or sprays of some sort, are a must for the flower arranger, and I have selected a few that not only give a good show in the garden, but are also good for cutting.

Forsythia is invaluable to the flower arranger for both its yellow flowers – which appear in spring, usually before the leaves – and its foliage.

Viburnum (*opulus*) – the guelder rose – is a particular favourite of mine, although all viburnums are well worth growing (some take up a lot of space). This one not only has maple-like dark green leaves and round heads of small white flowers (in May/June), but the leaves turn crimson in autumn accompanied by bunches of red berries.

Jasminum (*nudiflorum*) – or winter-flowering jasmine – al-though it loses its leaves, bears long spikes of yellow flowers from November through to March. Perfect sprays for arrangements.

Syringa, or lilac, must be the commonest, therefore most popular, flowering shrub. It thrives in town gardens, can be a border, a hedge, or bushy, and it produces fragrant single or double flowers of all colours.

Camellias are wonderful – they have rich green, glossy leaves and cup- or bowl-shaped flowers which range from white through all shades and tints of pink to glorious reds – and one of the camellias is the tea plant without which we Brits could not survive! My own favourite camellia is 'Inspiration', a beautiful deep rose pink.

Ribes (*sanguineum*) or flowering currant, despite its smell, is useful. If you pick branches before the buds break, the foliage opens very pale lime green, almost cream, which is very attractive in simple arrangements.

This is a very good example of a smallish town garden. There are no lawns to mow, and a clever use is made of paved and gravelled areas as background for a variety of interesting and colourful plants. Herbs in the foreground – among them chives with their marvellous purple ball flowers – grow well in town gardens, and many can be used in arrangements as well as in cooking. There are wonderful tall spikes of New Zealand flax (phormium tenax), irises, and day lilies (hemerocallis) towards the back of the border, and ground-hugging plants lapping out over the gravel.

Willow and hazel are both wonderful trees to grow if you have the room, especially the latter, corylus (*avellana* 'Contorta'). Also known as Harry Lauder's Walking Stick (for obvious reasons, if you remember the contortions of his major prop), it has twists and turns and marvellous shapes in its branches and twigs that are very useful in arrangements. It is very decorative in March with long yellow catkins like lambs' tails, and then produces its cobnuts later.

GREEN GARDEN PLANTS

These, as I've said, should have pride of place in the flower arranger's garden, and in the photograph on page 30 you'll see some of the green foliage plants I grow in my own garden. There is an enormous range, and you should try always to produce something tall, something round, and something trailing. *Wonderful* effects can be created with greens, and you should never be without them.

Hostas (see photograph opposite) come in over twenty varieties, their foliages ranging in size from 2 inches (5 cm) to 20 inches (50 cm) in length. They range in colour from lime green to deep blue-grey. I grow them both in borders and in containers – a good idea if you want to keep your garden 'on the move': wherever there is a gap, you can fill it with a pot of hostas. In the winter, lay the containers on their sides so that the plants do not ice up. I have managed to keep some hostas in the same containers in my northern garden for some twelve years now.

Alchemilla vulgaris (*mollis*), or ladies' mantle, isn't popular with everyone, as it can be invasive. To the flower arranger, though, it's good cover, its lime-green colour glows on the dullest day, and it flowers the whole summer through.

Nicotiana, the tobacco plant, does come in many flower colours, but I find the best is the 'Lime Green' which produces, as you might gather, green flowers as well as its large leaves.

Ferns are useful and very striking in any garden. The family is enormous, so you have a lot of choice. The one thing to remember is not to cut ferns too young for flower-arranging purposes. Wait for the brown spores to appear on the back of the fern fronds before picking.

Fatsia (*japonica*) is a very useful evergreen plant that produces large leathery hand-shaped leaves and, in late autumn, huge clusters of ball-shaped flowers.

Arum (*italicum* 'Pictum'), see opposite.

Euphorbia (*robiae*), see opposite.

Iris (*pseudacorus*), a true water iris, can range from 24 inches (60 cm) to 5 feet (1.5 metres) in height. It does bear good yellow flowers, but it is grown mostly for its yellow-green ribbed leaves.

Angelica, the green herbal plant whose young stems are candied for cake and pudding decorations, has wonderful yellow-green flower heads which are useful in arrangements.

Molucella (*laevis*), more commonly known as bells of Ireland or shell flowers, are, to me, one of Mother Nature's wonders. They have a tiny insignificant white flower, with a large, shell-like pale green bract which is what is of interest to the flower arranger.

Helleborus is a large family, but one of my favourites is *orientalis* (see page 44).

The hosta family – or plantain lilies as they are often known – come in many sizes and colours, and a selection are vital in my flower-arranging garden. This is hosta (fortunei 'Albopicta'). Established clumps can be left undisturbed for many years, and it's wonderful at the front of a border. It darkens quickly from its May colouring of clear yellow with a pale green edge, to these two shades of green, which can be so useful to the flower arranger. In July it bears slender spikes of bell-shaped lilac flowers.

There are a great number of euphorbias – one of the most familiar is the poinsettia or Christmas flower – and they come in all sizes and colours. This one, euphorbia (robiae), is very popular. It has very dark green rosettes of foliage for the whole year, then produces a lime green flower spike in late spring. This goes on through the summer and turns to its autumn colours later. A very useful plant indeed for the flower arranger.

Arum (italicum 'Pictum') is a very useful plant. It starts to throw up its 12-inch (30-cm) spears of glossy green and cream veined leaves before Christmas, and produces wonderfully marked foliage right through until the summer. The flowers – pale yellow-green and hooded in shape – appear in April/May, and can be used in arrangements; and in August, after the leaves die down, you get some very useful spikes of glowing orangey-red (but poisonous) berries.

GREY GARDEN PLANTS

Although greens are the most useful, grey foliage in a flower arranger's garden is almost as much a necessity. These silvery greys contribute so much to an arrangement's colouring, a sort of muted, smoky and subtle silver-grey.

Senecio is a shrub that comes immediately to mind. *Greyii* is easy to propagate from cuttings (and has wonderful yellow flowers in June/July), and *maritima* ('Silver Dust') survives annually in my northern garden, growing well from seed.

Artemisia, *ludoviciana* (white sage) or *lactiflora* (white mugwort), are both good for soft feathery grey and aromatic outline foliage.

Teucrium (*fruticans*) is one of my two favourite grey foliage plants. I find that it needs the boiling water treatment (see page 47) to make it stand well in an arrangement.

Helichrysum (*petiolatum*) is my other favourite. The stems and foliage, covered in a dense felt of white hairs, make beautiful curving shapes when cut.

PLANTS FOR DRYING

To make the most of plants grown in your flower arranger's garden, you could also grow things that can be dried. There are many things that can be grown in the border that not only will be useful in the fresh

The flower of helleborus (orientalis) – the Lenten rose – comes not only in green colours but also in white, cream, and shades of pink through to dark purple, almost black. Both this and the dark green leaves are of interest for the flower arranger. More familiar to many people may be helleborus (niger), the Christmas rose.

PLANTS FOR THE FLOWER ARRANGER'S GARDEN			
Green	**Yellow/Bronzes**	**Greys**	**Drying & Preserving**
Acanthus	Acacia	Agave	Acanthus
Alchemilla mollis	Acer	Artemisia	Achillia
Amaranthus	Balm	Artichoke	Acrolinium
Angelica	Berberis	Ballota	Allium
Arum	Cornus	Centaurea	Artichoke
Bergenia	Cotinus	Eucalyptus	Cortaderia
Buxus	Cytisus	Garrya elliptica	Delphinium
Camellia	Disanthus	Hedera	Dipsacus
Choisya ternata	Elaeagnus	Helichrysum	Echinops
Cotoneaster	Epimedium	Rosmarinus	Eryngium
Cupressus	Euonymus	Ruta	Gourds
Decorative kale	Euphorbia	Salix	Grasses
Escallonia	Forsythia	Santolina	Helichrysum
Euphorbia	Hamamelis mollis	Sedum	Limonium
Fatsia japonica	Hedera	Senecio	Lunaria
Ferns	Iris	Stachys lanata	Molucella
Hedera	Kerria japonica	Teucrium	Papaver
Helleborus	Ligustrum	Verbascum	Physalis
Hosta	Phlomis		Scirpus
Hypericum	Phormium tenax		
Iris	Sorbus		
Laurus	Viburnum		
Mahonia	Vitis coignetiae		
Molucella			
Nicotiana			
Phormium tenax			
Polygonatum			
Skimmia			
Tellima			
Weigela			
Yucca			
Zinnia			

state, but could produce good seed heads, or wonderful dried or preserved foliage. See also Chapter Eight.

Helichrysum (the straw or ever-lasting flower) is obvious.

Acroliniums are easy to grow, and are very popular with flower arrangers and non-flower arrangers alike. They (and helichrysum) can be tied in bunches (or bought in bunches from the florists) and simply hung for a few weeks to dry.

Eryngium (sea holly) is a good plant to grow for something blue.

Limonium (statice) comes in mixed colours for drying.

Achillea (yarrow) will be useful for a touch of yellow.

Papaver (*orientale*), or oriental poppy, is useful for its dried heads.

The onion or *allium* family not only look good for interest in the border while they are in flower, but supply useful heads in the autumn.

Cortaderia (pampas grass) used as a feature plant, if you have the space, is a must both for the strip-like foliage and, of course, for the plumes.

Dipsacus or teasels I have stopped growing in my own garden – they get everywhere when seeding – but kind friends grow them in their gardens for me!

Physalis (Chinese lantern or Cape gooseberry) is useful as well – I use it a lot – but it needs plenty of space because it is invasive. It doesn't shed its seeds as the teasel does, but creeps about underground and pops up where you least expect or want it.

CONDITIONING PLANT MATERIALS

Next to growing plant materials, conditioning is the most important step before attempting an arrangement. Conditioning is the process of giving extended life to your cut plant materials, and it can make a very great difference indeed to their arrangement life if done properly. If you've gone to all the trouble of arranging flowers beautifully, you want the arrangement to *last*! And to make it last when arranged, you must always make sure that there is a little water in the container around the floral foam. If you don't have this, the floral foam will become dry (therefore will not soak again), and the flowers will die. The amount of water needed, and the frequency of topping up, will depend on various factors – whether the room is centrally heated, for instance.

Some plant materials just *do* stand better than others when cut and, as with many aspects of the art, it's a question of experience, and you will quickly learn. All plant materials – flowers and foliages – when cut, will benefit from good clean conditioning, with *clean* water in a *clean* bucket. And the first rule to remember is to cut, pick or buy flowers or foliage the day before arranging, and to condition well before use.

GARDEN PLANT MATERIALS

Always cut plant materials in the early morning or late evening – which decreases the chances of them wilting. Although it may look good to the neighbours, don't equip yourself with a gathering basket or trug: take a few inches of water with you in the bottom of a plain, ordinary but clean, bucket. As the plant material is cut, it can go straight into the water and start conditioning immediately.

As for cutting, always use sharp scissors or secateurs, and cut the stem or branch on the slant.

This will expose a larger area of drinking surface, and does away with the risk of a straight-cut stem adhering to the bottom of the container, thus preventing any water at all getting up the stem. While you're at it, strip away the lower foliage. You'll probably remove it anyway when arranging, and if left on through the conditioning process, it could foul the water. Once cut, place the plant materials straight into the water. It's when they're left out of water that the trouble starts, when air locks form to stop the drinking process. Once all the required material has been cut, put the bucket in a cool place and top up the water level to two-thirds full. Leave for 12 hours minimum or overnight, and the plant materials will then be perfect for arranging.

Some plant materials, though, need some further treatment before they can take up the conditioning water successfully. There are two main methods – boiling and singeing the stem ends. Boiling is the method to use with woody stems – blossoms, roses, chrysanthemums etc – and wild flowers also seem to last just that bit longer. (But as with everything else in the art of flower-arranging, it's experience that will tell.) Put about 2 inches (5 cm) boiling water into a bucket and stand the re-cut stems in it for about 20 seconds. Keep the flower heads out of the steam if possible, and the water will remove any air lock and start the plant drinking again. Thereafter place the stems in deep cold water and leave for 12 hours or overnight.

Flowers like spurges, euphorbias, helleborus and tellima do better after a singeing treatment. The cut stem ends (which bleed a milky substance) need to be held over a flame – a candle or match – until scorched and sealed. They should then be plunged into the deep conditioning water for the 12 hours or overnight.

Don't forget that foliages too need to be conditioned in exactly the same way as flowers – cut, into the bucket, back to the house, and deep water overnight. Do, though, be careful with grey foliages, which could lose their bloom and greyness if completely submerged in water.

FLORISTS' PLANT MATERIALS

Many of the same rules apply with florists' flowers, and the first is to buy in good time to do the same conditioning. You don't know what treatment the florist has been able to give, so make sure by doing your own. If you are out shopping, don't buy the flowers first thing and leave them in your car or carry them from shop to shop. Buy them last on the shopping agenda, then rush home with them. After the kettle has gone on, re-cut all the stems and put into a bucket of cold clean water. Put in a cool place for at least 12 hours and then arrange.

I once asked a lady in a class of mine whose plant materials were not looking too good whether she had conditioned them before coming to class. She claimed proudly: 'They couldn't be fresher, I picked them on the way out'! I just didn't know what to say, other than they might have been freshly picked, but, without conditioning, they certainly weren't fresh for flower arranging. So always condition well, keep everything clean, prepare well in advance, make a good friend of your local florist – and you'll enjoy a long-lasting and beautiful display.

CHAPTER FOUR

FLOWERS
IN CHURCH

Decorating churches with flower arrangements must be one of the best and ultimate ways in which the flower arranger can express his or her talent. It doesn't matter whether it's a tiny village church or a cathedral, flowers decorate beautifully, bringing pleasure and giving thanks. But some basic rules must apply: the arrangements must suit the architecture and size of the building first of all. Traditional large pedestal arrangements look wonderful in large old churches, but something more stylised could look better in the new modern churches and cathedrals. I remember a few years ago standing in a modern cathedral imagining what I could do if let loose. I was looking at a rather small, traditional, pedestal arrangement at the time, and was asked by a lady standing nearby what I thought of the cathedral. 'Fantastic,' I enthused, 'but what a pity about the flowers.' I went into full flow: modern hessian-covered columns would have been better than the thin wrought-iron ones; groups of large branching foliage would have created a beautifully stark, modern outline. 'Interesting,' she said, 'do *you* arrange flowers?' I agreed that I did, just a little. 'Well,' she said, 'I'm an expert, and I arranged all these flowers.' I had come across one of those church flower ladies!

Which brings me onto a general point about working in churches.

Apart from being (hopefully) rather less tactless than I, get to know the people involved, the vicar, the verger, the ladies who do the arrangements; make yourself familiar with various aspects of the church organisation, like who holds the keys apart from verger and caretaker, and, most importantly, where the water supply is. It will make things very much more friendly and easy in the long run.

Other general principles involve the size of the building. You will be working in a huge area so, as suggested above, small arrangements will seldom be appropriate. Most church or cathedral flowers will be seen from a distance, too, so the arrangements must be larger, the flowers bolder, the outlines and shapes stronger. The height of the arrangements is important, too: the flowers should be seen, and with a great many people sitting and standing in a church, this means that they should be at least at waist height, if not higher. And with height and size, and thus heavier plant materials, you *must* make sure that your mechanics are really sturdy and firm. As I go through the various church celebrations and festivals, and illustrate them with relevant arrangements, you will see these principles applied, and will understand what I am getting at.

The final thing to remember is always to be tidy. Use a ground sheet, put any rubbish in plastic bags or a box, to take away with you, and find out from one of your

Twin pedestal arrangements in their final position on either side of the chancel, in front of the screen, where they act as a framework for the wedding ceremony. And as you look through the screen, the altar and its twin arrangements are clearly visible, smaller replicas of the pedestal arrangements. You can also appreciate why the shape of the altar arrangements had to be bold. (For step-by-step photographs, see page 54.)

The altar is the most important part of the church, especially during a wedding – nothing must detract from this fact – and so the arrangements should be fairly simple in concept. Don't forget that flowers on the altar will not be viewed closely, so a striking shape, a slender symmetrical effect, is the look to achieve. Small flowers will just disappear, so think big – use gladioli, carnations, chrysanthemums, dahlias, all larger and bolder in shape. I chose both spray and single bloom carnations with spray chrysanthemums, and arranged them in soaked floral foam in two low dish containers. Always remember, too, the 'rules' about arranging twin containers: do both simultaneously.

church friends where the brush and shovel are kept. When you make a return visit to arrange flowers, you'll be remembered with warmth if you cleaned up afterwards; if you left bits and pieces all up the aisle and chancel steps, they'll remember that too . . .

WEDDINGS

When asked to arrange flowers for a wedding, whether for money or love, there will be a certain amount of prior organisation. The first consideration is that of budget. The number of arrangements will depend upon the simplicity or elegance of the wedding, but primarily on cost. If money is limited, a couple of large arrangements in imposing positions will look much more impressive than bitty little arrangements scattered here and there. If money is not so limited, you could have fun with many of the ideas suggested in the following pages.

The second thing of importance when dealing with the bridal party is the colour scheme of the wedding. There is no point in creating a pink and white extravaganza if the bride's attendants are all in orange. White may be their preference – it is mine, as well as being the colour most traditionally associated with weddings – but if you know the church, and think a little warm colour could make all the difference (white is cold), never be afraid to say so. Always be firm in your recommendations, and point out anything you think will not be right. I've been asked many times for instance, to do arrangements at a low level, even on the floor, and I've never hesitated to say that to use those areas would be a waste of money, time and effort. They will

look lovely in the empty church, but will completely disappear from view when the church is full of people.

The next thing to do is familiarise yourself with the church, its personnel and all the timings involved. Make sure you won't be stepping on the toes of the lady on the flower rota. Check with the vicar about other weddings on the same day; if there are other weddings, sometimes the various parties can get together either completely, or at least to sort out a colour scheme that suits everyone. (Also check a couple of days before the wedding that there isn't going to be a funeral on the wedding morning – it can happen, and has.) Tell the bridal party and the vicar where you are tentatively planning to put your arrangements – there seems to be a trend against flowers on the altar nowadays, for instance – and enquire about any existing containers or stands which you might be able to use.

As most weddings take place on a Saturday, start preparing mid week. Get together all the mechanics side of the flower arrangements – the floral foam, the containers you plan to use, any accessories, as well as your tool box (don't forget that ground sheet). Pick and prepare your foliage early, as foliage comes to no harm with two to three days in conditioning water. Pick and buy the required flowers on Thursday and condition well (see Chapter Three). Arrange them on Friday at the church: in fact you could even leave them to condition at the church if space is at a premium at home. I would never advise that the arranging was left until the Saturday, or the day of the wedding, as you never know what might happen – the car might not

start, for instance. And if you can, check on the day itself that the flowers look all right, that they haven't started wilting: they *must*, and should, of course, look their best (and they haven't been paid for yet either).

The church I chose for the photographs of wedding flowers is local to me – St Mary's, Luddenden, West Yorkshire – and it is a delightful country church, a joy to work in.

THE ALTAR

If altar arrangements are approved, check whether brass altar vases are a permanent fixture – the donors or their families may be offended if you move them. They are traditional, I know, but not the easiest of containers to deal with. In the past, they were perfect receptacles for a single stem of lilies or a few flowers with a little fern as foliage, but I much prefer to use low dish containers on lifts or boxes – as in the twin arrangements on page 50. If you have to use the brass vases, the best solution is to cut a piece of soaked floral foam into a cone shape, put some water in the vase, and then wedge the cone into the vase, point down, so that you have the wide end uppermost into which to make your arrangement.

The only time I've really appreciated flowers in brass altar vases was when my wife and I visited the hill town of Monti in Madeira. I had never seen such a beautifully decorated altar as in that delightful cathedral. Fifty or sixty brass vases – there must be a large number of donors in Madeira – were grouped between the cross and candlesticks, over the altar table and onto the steps, holding nothing but sprays of white camellia.

Basically, though, the altar is spiritually the centre and the focal point of the church, and the flowers should both be large enough to be seen from afar, and simple enough not to detract from the altar itself.

WINDOWSILLS AND LEDGES

Obvious places for flowers, but they can be difficult because of the stained glass colours and the back light (see page 66 for a ledge arrangement that I think worked very well). Flat windowsills are no problem with a flat container, but many church sills are sloping. If there is time, a wedge-shaped piece of wood can be affixed to your container to bring it level; if all else fails, a block of floral foam wrapped in clingfilm will take an arrangement, but will have to be anchored somehow. Circumstances vary so much that it's difficult to advise – but flower arrangers are very inventive, and you're bound to come up with something!

Boldness should be the key for windowsill or ledge flowers, with plenty of background greenery.

PEDESTALS

Of all the arrangements for church, the pedestal is *the* traditional arrangement. Most pedestal arrangements should be symmetrical or asymmetrical in shape, with a clear-cut design: don't go for gimmicks. I prefer pedestals with just a platform on the top, which allows you to use the size of bowl that you like, and will take the size of arrangement that suits the occasion. Many commercial pedestals have a fixed bowl which just is not large enough most of the time. If a large amount of plant material is being used in the pedestal arrangement, a good-sized container is essential.

If budget allows, I would always prefer to do two pedestal arrangements, at the chancel steps, or at either side of the screen. This is where the wedding service is taking place, it's where all the guests will be looking, and the arrangements will act as a frame for the wonderful picture of the bridal couple and their attendants. In the photograph on page 48, you will see the pedestals – with a strong bold shape and an elegant flow – framing the distant altar and echoing the shape of its simple arrangements.

The one thing to remember when working with twin arrangements – and I cannot emphasise this enough – is to do the pair simultaneously. I mean this literally – outline in one, and then outline in the other, stage by stage: it's the only way you will get a near-matching pair.

FONTS

Fonts come in all shapes and sizes and in all positions in the church, some tucked away in a corner, others in a very prominent position. Most, though, are near the doors, and thus make a wonderful receptacle for flowers. The bridal party and wedding guests will probably have to go out that way, so it's good that they have a lovely arrangement to look at. And if the bridal party are hogging the porch for photographs, it will be something rather nice for the waiting guests to look at. Find out first from the vicar whether he minds you doing an arrangement in the font: you never know, they may need the font on Sunday for a christening. To solve that problem, use another container inside the font – I use a washing-up bowl – and thus all that has to be done is to lift the complete arrangement out.

1. *Applying the principles of flower arranging (which you now know so well), make a good strong foliage outline into the soaked floral foam in the container of the pedestal. I used sprays of beech for the vertical and thin sweeps to the side, with large ferns, ivy (hedera canariensis) and large hosta leaves for weight, texture and hiding the mechanics. The arrangement already has a good bold shape.*

2. *(far right) The next stage is to strengthen the outline, which I have done with gladioli, spray chrysanthemums and, to give weight towards the centre, heads of rhododendron. At this stage, you can see how the arrangement shape is forming, with the principal elements already established – bold outline, flow and a good heart or focal point.*

3. *The next step is the filling in, which I have done with white spray carnations and, as you can see, there are still gaps, particularly towards the centre.*

4. *(far right) To complete the arrangement, I added bridal pink roses which finally unite and bring together all the colours and shapes of the composition.*

See page 48 for the finished arrangements.

I decided to do my harvest festival arrangement in the porch of St Mary's, Luddenden. For the arrangement itself, because of the weight of plant material, I used a large, heavy metal container holding soaked floral foam with wire mesh stretched and fixed across the top. The outline was started with long sweeping sprays of mountain ash (sorbus scalaris), ivy (hedera canariensis) and hop (homulus lupulus). The centre weight was created with large hosta leaves. The spiky outline flowers are yellow gladioli to give colour, height and width, and the pale orange carnations and orange lilies ('Enchantment') are grouped to give a bolder colour. To soften, and to bring the arrangement together, pale orange pompon and large cactus dahlias were used, but I still felt some further interest was needed. I added sprays of physalis (Cape gooseberries) and some wired-together bunches of corn.

To decorate the font for a wedding, I decided to do a duo group, rather than one actually in the font. I didn't want either to hide the beauties of the old carved stone font, so the secondary group was placed at the foot, to take the eye down, to make it follow the lines of the font and its interest. The ledges around the top and foot of the font were wide enough to take flat-bottomed containers with the taped and soaked floral foam. I decided to make the top arrangement follow the bowl shape – so that on close inspection the font bowl could still be seen – and used the same colouring, textures and flowers as in the pedestal arrangements: gladioli, rhododendrons, carnations and spray chrysanthemums. The foliages again are hosta and fern.

Again, it's a matter of being bold. In most cases, fonts are large stone or marble containers, so you mustn't be twee, you have all that mass to fight against. Have a look at my font arrangements – I chose to do two – opposite. The flowers are bold, the shapes interesting, and you can still see the beauties of the font itself.

Sometimes money does not allow the font to be decorated – it takes a lot of flowers – but some wonderful effects can be created in other ways. What about all foliage? Sprays of beech, fern and hosta, as in the pedestal arrangement outline, could look super. I remember doing a font a few years ago, and it cost me nothing at all except a little time collecting and conditioning. I filled the font with cow parsley or anthriscus and may (hawthorn) blossom, and it looked fantastic. (Some consider both are unlucky, and if you are worried, arrange them with your fingers crossed!) And in the autumn, a font can be decorated with all those wonderful colours and again lovely long sprays of the hawthorn with their berry fruit (the bread-and-cheese tree we called it as children). Mother Nature has provided all these joys so why not let us use them.

PEW ENDS

At one time, these were my least favourite arrangements because they were so difficult to fix on the pew. I can remember on one occasion getting my piece of cling film-wrapped floral foam attached somehow to the pew with sticky tape and blind faith: the more flowers I prodded into the foam the further down the pew end the foam slipped. A 4-inch (10-cm) nail made its appearance at the same time as the vicar; more frustration as the

nail's use was firmly vetoed. How things have changed. Holders have now been produced which do away with all that frustration: flat-backed plastic boxes with spikes take the floral foam; they can be arranged on a flat table surface just like any ordinary flower arrangement; and once completed, the arrangement is just hung over the pew end from a plastic hook! I used one of these containers in the photograph of a finished pew-end arrangement on page 58, and you can see that there is no hint of mechanics or slippage.

Do remember, though, that pew-end arrangements must not be too large, especially if the aisle is narrow. I will tell you how to make ribbon bows like the ones in the arrangement on page 98.

GARLANDS

Garlands can be delightful wedding decorations; they are also splendid at Christmas, and you can see them illustrated alongside the Christmas dining table in Chapter Seven. They can be put along the choir stalls, between or around pillars, or over the doors, and for a wedding foliage alone could suffice splendidly.

Long tubes of polythene can be bought and used for garland making. Soak blocks of floral foam, and cut into four lengthways. Thread the pieces of soaked foam into the tubing and use flexible ties between each piece, ending up with a long flexible sausage. Lay this sausage on the floor and use conditioned foliage cut into 5-inch (12.5-cm) lengths. Prod the polythene with the foliage in a lying down position so that each piece overlaps the piece before, thus hiding all the polythene and floral foam. Let the garland stand (or should I say lie)

Pew end arrangements for weddings look wonderful, but one thing to remember is not to make them too large or too wide, so that they protrude into the aisle. If the aisle is narrow, guests will have difficulty getting into their seats, and the bride might end up carrying more than one bouquet! Special plastic containers hold the floral foam and the arrangement, and are then simply hung over the pew end. I used sprays of ivy, leather fern and alchemilla (mollis) to create the background, with bows of white ribbon and trailers to complete the group. The flowers are now inserted into the floral foam, and they are spray and single bloom carnations and spray chrysanthemums ('Bonnie Jean').

until all surplus water has drained away, and then suspend in the desired way.

Although this method allows the foliage to last well, a quicker, easier method is to cut your conditioned foliage into 4–5-inch (10–12.5-cm) lengths, and bind these onto an old washing line. Attach the end of the line to a convenient nail, and have your supply of cut foliage ready, with a reel of florists' wire. Pick up individual pieces of foliage, lay on the washing line, and bind on with the wire. You will find yourself walking backwards – don't panic, this is quite normal – because as the garland progresses, you too are progressing backwards. You could go on for ever, of course, but remember to measure the lengths of rope you need before you start binding. The thing that I like about these rope garlands, is that they are easy to do, and they drape beautifully.

CHRISTENINGS

Flowers for a christening are, I think, a must – but something simple is needed, though, not the glorious extravagances associated with weddings. I prefer to leave the font clear of flowers, both around the rim and at the foot. There is so much going on there, and I think to have the added distraction of flowers would not help things go well. I have seen small arrangements dotted around the rim, and garlands of flowers making a complete collar. How some people expect the priest or vicar to control what could be a little wriggler as well as avoiding floating flowers and flower arrangements, I don't know!

An arrangement set near to the font or possibly on a windowsill nearby would be far better. I chose an interesting wrought-iron stand on which to do a free-standing arrangement (see opposite). It is similar to a pedestal, and is the ideal container for people who cannot handle large plant material – the effect will come from the massing together of the smaller arrangements. Standing on good firm feet, the branching arms with containers on the end can be revolved around the central column, thus it is an arrangement to be viewed from all sides.

This container that I used for the delicate christening arrangement has been very useful on many other church occasions. At Easter for instance, I thought it looked wonderful arranged with ivy sprays, forsythia blossom, mixed daffodils and narcissi. Very inexpensive to do, but so effective. At Christmas, the five containers hold mixed groups of variegated holly, cupressus, and pine foliage. Colour

Simplicity should be the keynote at a christening, and I think the font should be the last place to consider for your floral decorations. I chose to do tall delicate arrangements in an interesting wrought-iron stand with branching arms. Floral foam was fixed into each of the five containers with floral foam tape. For the outline of each arrangement, natural flowing material was used: sprays of ivy and alchemilla (mollis) keep the outline delicate, as does gypsophila ('Bristol Fairy', known as baby's breath in the United States, so rather appropriate for a christening arrangement). Single and spray carnations are the main flowers, with a few recessed spray chrysanthemums ('Bonnie Jean') to finish off the group.

is introduced by bows of velvet ribbon, sparkling glass baubles, and a few red spray carnations. The final effect is almost like a Christmas tree – but there are no dropping needles! See later in this section for some further Christmas ideas for churches.

HARVEST FESTIVALS

This must be *the* time for the church and for the flower arranger. It's saying thank-you for all the abundance of natural goodness and beauty, and no one can be more involved with those than the flower arranger. All those colours of autumn – flowers, leaves, fruits and berries – how could you not enjoy putting them together? In a large group, dried and preserved materials can also be used, and never forget how visually exciting and decorative are vegetables, fruits, eggs and breads. This is the *natural* time to use them – an opportunity I for one never pass up – but if you are a trifle hesitant about doing an arrangement with these items, just think back to your first hesitant step with flowers. You are still using forms, textures, and beautiful colourings, you are still using natural plant materials.

Have a look at my harvest festival composition in the porch of St Mary's, Luddenden, on page 55. The lovely stone pillar was already there in position and, as I could not move it, there it had to stay – but how beautiful with the stained glass to one side and the background of old grey stonework. To complement a more traditional flower arrangement, I have grouped some baskets which give a feel of plenty – which is, after all, what harvest festival is all about. The baskets add an autumny feel as

well, but they *must* look natural and not too contrived. This sort of accessory must be placed casually to give the right feeling. Although not to be recommended in many other arrangements, you want here to aim for a sort of natural 'spillage' effect! One basket holds a selection of vegetables with their wonderful colours, forms and textures; another holds some fruit and loaves of bread. The bunches of corn and the flowers echo the main flower group – togetherness! – and the old wine flagons just seem to pull it all together.

Finally, when composing such large arrangements as this, you must remember to have good firm mechanics and containers. And always remember to tie your ideas in with the festival theme: the local autumnal plenty, the colours – don't, for instance, introduce any exotics like bananas or pineapples – they'd be inappropriate. Sprays of blackberries, on the other hand, would look just right.

CHRISTMAS

I am always amazed that people who organise church flowers do not use more natural Christmas trees: a pair of beautifully shaped trees in tubs crowned with sumptuous red ribbon bows could look most impressive placed either side of the chancel steps. If that were not feasible, they could make their own 'trees'. Ball-shaped trees – like clipped bay trees – are so easy to do, and could look as effective as natural trees.

As with a flower arrangement, the mechanics have to be right first. You'll need a large plant pot, about 10 inches (25 cm) high, quick-drying cement, a broom handle, some pebbles or gravel, 4-inch (10-cm)

This Christmas arrangement was positioned near the pulpit and stands on an old oak stool. A good heavy flat-bottomed container holds two blocks of soaked floral foam, firmly taped in. The mechanics for this arrangement had to be particularly firm because of the weight of the candles – about 4 lb (1.8 kilos). The candles were placed first, anchored in with the aid of a trio of short canes. For each candle, three 5-inch (12.5-cm) lengths of cane were taped with floral foam tape to the base and sides, with half the cane length protruding below the candle. This 'tripod' pushes easily into the floral foam and holds the candles firmly. The flowing line on each side of the candles was then created with lovely sprays of variegated holly, Western hemlock (tsuga heterophylla), and sweet bay (laurus nobilis). A large double red ribbon bow was then centred and fifteen bright scarlet carnations completed the arrangement, echoing the reds of the background stained glass.

nails, paint and floral foam. Knock the nails opposite each other into the broom handle, about 1½ inches (3–4 cm) from the top end. Fill the pot with cement, and while it is still wet, push the broom handle home into the centre, the nails still at the top. Cover the cement with pebbles or gravel to give a more natural effect and leave to set and dry. Paint the 'trunk' of your tree either dark green or brown, then wrap half a block of soaked floral foam in clingfilm. Push this onto the top end of the broom handle to rest on the nails, and your mechanics are ready.

Cupressus, buxus and holly foliage will make a good ball shape. Prepare this well by conditioning in water for at least 12 hours, and cut into approximately 8-inch (20-cm) lengths. Cut with a slanting cut, which will help the stems go easily through the clingfilm and into the floral foam. Place the foliage all round the floral foam until you have a good round ball shape. Glass sparkling baubles, flower and bows of ribbon attached to stub wires, could then bring colour into the green foliage ball. A bow of ribbon with long trailers looks good on the under side of the ball with the trailers cascading down the broom handle trunk.

When the festivities are over, don't throw the pot and broom handle 'tree' away. Easter and other festivals will soon follow, and they can be useful again.

But other arrangements are also relevant at Christmas, and I always think red colours and candles are most appropriate.

See the photograph on page 61 for another festive idea, and of course see Chapter Seven for many more ways in which to celebrate at home.

CHURCH FLOWER FESTIVALS

Flower festivals have become part of the life of flower clubs and of their local churches, chapels and cathedrals. The main idea behind a flower festival is not just to bring joy to visitors but, usually, to produce large amounts of money to help the fabric repairs of the church. I have been involved in many festivals over the past few years, and find them most enjoyable. There are two sides to church flower festivals – the organisation and the actual flower arranging.

ORGANISATION

Although many people think that there isn't much to organise – we'll just put some flowers here, and some there, and that will do – there is in fact quite a lot involved. The first thing to do, of course, is to have a meeting with the vicar or priest at a very early stage, to discuss the possibilities, to let him know what a flower festival is all about, and to inform him of how much cooperation will be needed from the officers of the church in the way of publicity, stewarding, car parking and brochure printing. Refreshments too are very important, both on the staging day and throughout the length of the festival, and a ladies' committee from the church could probably look after that side.

A chairperson and a small committee from the flower club should then do the planning of the actual flower festival, visiting the church on a few occasions to familiarise themselves with the personnel and the building. This planning should be done well in advance: it cannot be done in a week, and a large flower festival

The delightful hill village of Heptonstall, West Yorkshire, is one of only six places in the British Isles where there are two churches in one churchyard. The functioning church of St Thomas à Beckett is nineteenth century, the ruins of the earlier church are thirteenth century. And it was amidst these ruins that I chose to display my simple arrangement of wild flowers on a pedestal, as an echo of the history of the churchyard itself. All the flowers were picked from around the churchyard; I popped them straight into the bucket of water I carried with me, and arranged them 12 hours later. I used crumpled wire netting and clean water in the container, as wild flowers do not seem to like floral foam. The outline height was created by fireweed (epilobium angustifolium, and also known as rosebay willowherb). To the sides, I used grasses, ferns, sedges, dock (rumex), and easterledge (polygonum bistorta). The centre was made up of yellow hawkweed (hieracium).

During the early part of the nineteenth century, the church of St Thomas à Beckett was struck by lightning, part of the tower ending up in the graveyard. I decided to use this lightning strike as my festival theme, and some of the fallen masonry as the focal point of the grouping. Using two metal pedestal containers – one level with the tallest column, one a little higher than the smaller column – I taped in my floral foam. The lightning strikes, two large branches of African thorn, form the 'verticals', with a further branch spiking out below. The foliages used were green beech, ferns, ivy (hedera canariensis) and hosta. The flowers in the top are blue-grey gladioli, blue hydrangeas, yellow roses and lilies ('Connecticut King'). This yellow flows down into the middle arrangement, with the yellow lilies again and spray carnations. Here red starts to be introduced with 'Baccarat' roses, and it cascades down into the third element with red carnations and red gladioli. The colours echo those of the church's stained glass, and the slightly zig-zag effect of the three arrangements emphasises the basic lightning theme.

could take months. Once a plan has been agreed by the committee, it should then be put to the priest for his approval. One or two of the places you thought flowers might look good, he may not like.

The *theme* of the flower festival should then be considered once everyone has agreed on the basics. Is the church celebrating any particular anniversary? Is there something special happening locally? Some churches, abbeys and cathedrals have such beautiful stonework, woodwork and stained glass: could a flower festival be arranged around these elements – glass blowing, woodcarving and the stone mason? Many churches have famous or historical people associated with them, and this again could be a good subject for a flower festival. Passages from the Bible have often been used as themes, and this is a very fruitful source.

But it is often the history of a church that is the most obvious, especially when the whole festival is being staged in aid of the church itself. In the photographs on pages 63 and 64, you can see my two quite different interpretations of aspects of the history of the church of St Thomas à Beckett in Heptonstall, West Yorkshire. The wild flower arrangement, simple and subtle, is a reflection of the natural beauty gleaned from the ruins of the thirteenth-century church; and the lightning strike arrangement, actually using parts of the masonry damaged by that strike, directly echoes that particular part of the church's history.

FLOWER FESTIVAL ARRANGING

I have been involved in many church flower festivals – at York Minster, St Paul's Cathedral, Ripon Cathedral and Westminster Abbey, apart from most chapels and churches in Yorkshire. The one that will always stand out in my mind took place in Westminster Abbey in 1977. When I was chosen to be one of the arrangers, my only request was, could I stand on my own two feet to do the arrangement that was being planned for me. I had done so many arrangements for these occasions where I was up a ladder, hanging over a ledge, or swinging around on a rope, that I felt it was time I kept my feet on the ground! I did in fact get an arrangement I could reach from the floor, but it was to be 10 feet (3 metres) high and 12 feet (3.6 metres) long! Representing the 'nobles of the past', it was in glorious colourings – reds, purples and golds. You can see in the photograph below what I mean about height!

And the next step, once the plans have been set and approved by the whole committee and the priest or vicar, is to decide who is to do what. In all flower clubs there

Perhaps one of the disadvantages of being a male flower arranger is that I always seem to be asked to do the high arrangements. In this photograph, taken in St Thomas à Beckett, Heptonstall, I am up a ladder working on a ledge about 20 feet (6 metres) above the floor! It was an obvious position to set an arrangement, at the top of an arched doorway, above a painting of 'The Last Supper', and beneath a magnificent stained-glass window.

Now that you have a closer idea of the scale involved, you'll understand the need for a large arrangement and for larger, bolder flowers. As a container, I used a large plastic washing-up bowl which took six blocks of soaked floral foam, leaving only a little space for extra water. Very large sprays of green beech form the foliage outlines, and the flowers are mixed gladioli in creams, oranges and reds. The finished arrangement measured about 10 feet (3 metres) across and 6 feet (1.8 metres) in height.

will be the very experienced members who can always be relied upon to do an efficient job and a beautiful arrangement, but never forget that new members should always be included as well. There is scope for every willing helping hand, and a little encouragement goes a long way. A nice little position for a smaller size arrangement can always be found, and in time they will all move on to larger things! Give everyone who is taking part a detailed idea of what is required of them: decide where their space is to be, what sort of design would be best, as well as its size, and what colourings would suit the themes of the arrangements. For the experienced arranger such details can be minimal, but beginners will appreciate as much help as possible.

As a final thought on the subject of flower festivals and possible themes, I did an arrangement in the church of St Thomas à Beckett which combined both a church theme and a celebration of the newly founded World Association of Flower Arrangers. I fixed the arrangement to the organ gallery – another church position which you can consider (see below). With its profusion of 'international' dried plant materials, it was a tribute to the many flower arrangers all over the world.

I hope that your flower festival will be successful, and do remember on the de-staging day, to leave the church in a good clean state, and to thank all the members of the flower club and the church members for their help.

In 1984 WAFA got off the ground, and I wished to celebrate this as one of my themes in church flower festival arrangements and include some of the plant materials I had collected in my travels as a flower arranger. St Thomas à Beckett had some wonderful examples of vergers' staves, so I decided to incorporate them too. I fixed the staves securely to the front of the organ gallery with floral foam tape, and where they crossed over in the centre, I fixed two blocks of styrofoam. Into this I made the dried arrangement with proteas from South Africa, banksia from Australia, grape leaves from the USA, aspidistra from Malta, poppy heads from Belgium, giant bean pods from Kenya, molucella from Ireland, and artichokes from the British Isles.

CHAPTER FIVE

FROM COTTAGE TO CASTLE

Natural plant materials decorate a room beautifully, giving life to it, whether it be cottage or castle, and this chapter will deal with many different types of arrangement. The emphasis, however, is on matching your arrangements, materials, containers, theme, *feel*, to your moods, personal tastes, and the setting of your home. Every home is different, and everyone's ideas of colour and background environment vary widely; 'taste' must be first and foremost – for everyone has taste: their own!

When it comes to planning a flower arrangement in your home, whether it be an old stone cottage, a modern apartment, a Georgian mansion or indeed a castle, plan it so that it looks at home, both in size and colour, and in design. It should never dominate, but be part of the room's setting. In this chapter I explore simpler arrangements and their relevance to a number of settings; I show how I have managed to create a eastern feel in arrangements; I sing the praises of fruit, vegetables and berries used decoratively; and I display the large massed arrangements I was inspired to create by the beauties of my 'castle', Harewood House in Yorkshire.

SIMPLER THEMES

The art of flower arranging is still comparatively new in the modern western world, but it is constantly growing in popularity. I never cease to be surprised, though, that so many western homes do not utilise flower arrangements more: for their ability to transform a room setting, to bring freshness into it, to complement its decor, merely to decorate, can contribute so much to life and beauty. One of the most delightful aspects of a flower arrangement in the home is its infinite capacity for variation, and in the photograph on page 70, you can see how a simple basket of wild flowers brings colour and vitality to a window ledge and to the room.

This arrangement would not have been suitable for your castle, of course, but its simple lines should open your eyes to the possibilities. If you come to love flower arranging as I do, you will open both your heart and mind to it. You will not restrict yourself to just one style or method, but you will respect the principles and 'rules'. You will teach your fingers the techniques, becoming gradually more competent and more instinctive about the art. You will always work out what you have to offer the setting of the room, and get to know when the flower arrangement feels 'at home'. As you familiarise yourself with the settings in your home, looking at them from that new point of view, you will start to acquire that creativity, and *know* that when it looks right to you, it *is* right. The photograph opposite, again of a simple arrangement in a basket, shows this well.

If a flower arrangement is designed to suit its setting, if it says, 'I feel at home here', it will look right. Here in an old cottage, with a background of leaded windows and blue and white china, the arrangement in the large gathering basket looks natural and comfortable. Although sophisticated flowers such as carnations and gerberas are the main flowers used, the basket allows the arrangement to retain its essential informality. Other flowers and foliages are escallonia, begonia (rex, the large leaves in the centre, borrowed from a house plant), and gypsophila ('Bristol Fairy'). The same flowers and foliages, and the same essential arrangement, would look as good in a grand bronze container, say – but it would have to be included in the right setting.

Here, in a simple trug basket, I have arranged wild flowers collected from the field over my garden fence: buttercups, dandelions, daisies and varied grasses. The major thing to remember when using wild flowers is their careful preparation. Carry a bucket of water with you and start them conditioning immediately they are picked. Arrange them 12 hours later, and try to use wire mesh and water only, rather than floral foam.

Although the flowers are more sophisticated, the basket lends the group an informality that blends with the wood and stone of the cottage background. The same flowers and arrangement would look good in a grander container than the basket, but it would have to be matched to a different, its own, setting. And in a Japanese home, for instance, with its quiet angular lines and cool uncluttered settings, this pink arrangement would look quite out of place. In a modern, light-painted flat or a stone cottage, though, the simple lines of the arrangement opposite, with its pottery accessories, would look just right.

EASTERN THEMES

In Japan, flower arranging – Ikebana – has been part of the way of life for generations, and although I am not qualified to either do or write about Ikebana arrangements, I occasionally like to introduce their sparse, oriental *feeling* into my work. Again, suit the theme and its interpretation to its setting. The arrangement on page 72 was inspired by the beautiful curves of the French cabinet, and although these fan shapes could look good in a more modern setting, that element of 'togetherness' is particularly evident here.

The 'drainpipe' arrangement

The setting here, the bare walls and stonework of an old cottage, calls for a simple line and theme. The two stone jugs and the plate come from Kenya, but as they echo the lines and colours of their setting, they look at home. In soaked floral foam in a small container, the outline was created by simple foliages – iris (pseudacorus) and some extra height from dried grasses. Sprays of polygonatum (Solomon's seal), which look like giant lily of the valley, were stripped of their leaves, and flow to the sides. Large hosta leaves ('Thomas Hogg') give some weight towards the base, as do the bunches of grapes.

A flower arrangement can suggest many personalities, and should always be designed to suit the mood of a room. In this arrangement, I have tried to create an eastern feeling, but I was inspired first by the curves of the beautiful French cabinet, which, in turn, suggested the inclusion of the linen fans from China. The furniture demanded a more traditional treatment than, say, the arrangement using column containers, opposite, which is for a more modern setting. As the fans had bamboo staves, I made the arrangement in a tiny, low bamboo side table, both to echo the bamboo and to act as support. The fans slotted easily between the table struts, and then I positioned two containers, one between and one in front of the fans. The soaked floral foam holds the outline foliage of deep bronze prunus – note the line created by the spray flowing outwards and down – and the central foliage is hosta (fortunei 'Albopicta'). Nine pale pink carnations flowing from the top to the foot of the arrangement complete the picture.

This arrangement – still continuing the oriental theme, but designed for a more modern setting – shows how a little ingenuity and work can create unusual and striking containers. These columns are not expensive hand-thrown pottery, but cheap and made at home from two lengths of grey plastic fall pipe from the plumber's yard. I cut mouth shapes into them with a hacksaw, and to create the levels and to support the floral foam, I glued margarine cartons inside the tubes below the mouths. I then covered the tubes with a strong paste solution and rolled them in sand sprinkled on a large sheet of polythene. When dry, I securely glued on a design using rope washing line, and when dry again, I repeated the paste and sand process. The effect is interesting, and the columns make ideal containers for a fairly simple but striking outline of green beech with ivy (hedera canariensis) as the recessed foliage and cream lilies for shape and colour.

I'm a great believer in utilising the glorious shapes, colours and textures of vegetables and fruit in arrangements, and there are many examples of these throughout the book. But here, in a corner of my kitchen, you can see how decorative vegetables are, without actually being arranged in any formal way. The simple basket, holding peppers, carrots, cauliflower, marrow, leeks, parsnips and tomatoes with beans in front (a working arrangement?!), looks magnificent, bringing colour, texture and interest to the kitchen, especially with the background of glass and all its reflections. Note the unusual use of modern spaghetti jars. I have filled them with dried beans and pulses to look rather like those coloured Alum Bay sand containers from the Isle of Wight. A decoration in themselves, they look much more interesting than spaghetti! The other glass container is an old whisky jar.

on page 73, which carries on the eastern theme, is obviously far more suited to the plainer lines of a modern setting. And indeed the home-made container of this arrangement will, I hope, inspire you to think about different shapes, forms and textures, and inspire you to start thinking about creating your own containers. If you want to achieve a certain effect, you will probably have to start 'inventing' in your spare time. I started to do this purely because I never could find what I wanted or needed.

USING FRUIT AND VEGETABLES

As I've said several times, I'm very enthusiastic about fruit and vegetables, and their use as decoration. I've shown my collections of shells and glass, and how effective they look grouped together in the simplest and most informal way – but why not use fruit and vegetables similarly? In the photograph opposite, you will see a simple grouping of vegetables which, because of their varying shapes and colours, look decorative and create interest in the corner of a room which is too often neglected as far as plant material arrangements are concerned – and vegetables and kitchens go so naturally together.

The history of art shows that vegetables and fruit have always been an intrinsic part of life. The forms and shapes of cucumbers, pumpkins, apples and tomatoes, have made their appearance in many works of art over the centuries, in both paintings and sculpture, and although this amply demonstrates that these forms and shapes can truly be the medium of the artist, and thus of the flower arranger, I have found it difficult to

persuade colleagues that fruit and vegetables can be just as beautiful and interesting to work with as flowers. Many years ago, at a national flower arrangement festival, there was a competitive class for vegetables and foliage, and I still think it was one of the best classes I have seen.

If you are hesitant about doing your first design with fruit and vegetables, remember that you were probably as hesitant with your first flower arrangement; remember that you are still manipulating shapes, forms and textures and, of course, beautiful colourings. As you try to get colour, form, shape, interest, texture and a talking point into a flower arrangement, so you should aim for the same qualities in an arrangement of fruit and vegetables. When you begin, remember that the particular shape you use has a particular function. Just as in a flower arrangement, cylinder and pointed shapes give height and width; round and disc shapes contribute weight towards the centre; small fruits and vegetables such as radishes can be made into groups and clusters. It's all a matter of creating variation, and you should aim for as much as possible, because repetition becomes monotonous. Vary the size as well as the amounts: different sizes of the same type also add interest.

Just as you would for a flower arrangement, select a colour for dominance. For instance, if you choose scarlet, there are peppers, tomatoes, red apples, bronze grapes and a cut watermelon. Use a smaller amount of the secondary fruits and vegetables thereafter to avoid taking over from the main colour grouping. Scale is also most important in the design, and before

Here in this informal group, I have used a modern pine table which has an interesting hand-carved bowl in its top. I didn't want to use the bowl as a container – its textural interest would have been lost – so situated the arrangement to the side. The central interest is the small watermelon, a slice cut away to show both the skin and the pink flesh. This pink colouring has been carried further by the use of plums, red apples and the red/yellow nectarine. Lime green apples soften the group colours and help to bring in the pineapple and the yellow-skinned melon at the back of the group, which give further weight. The whole design comes together with the mixed greens – the small curly cucumbers, the marrows and green peppers – and, of course, the foliage, mixed hosta leaves.

buying your items, look at the sizes: don't buy oranges and apples all of one size, for instance. Remember too that texture and form are of primary importance to the design. Heavy textured vegetables such as pumpkins are best suited to a more informal arrangement, whereas the glossy skin of a melon will suit a more refined setting.

The collection of fruits and vegetables grouped on a modern pine table in the photograph below helps to illustrate this point. It also shows the importance of foliage when arranging fruit. Foliage helps to break up the tendency to have too many round shapes, as well as giving a natural appearance to the arrangement. Although many people would not want to combine both fruits and vegetables – the latter convey more a feeling of casualness, while fruits are more refined – both can offer endless possibilities. The lushness of bunches of grapes, the powdered

bloom on plums, the shiny texture of peppers, give a wide range of surface qualities which help you to compose a formal or informal arrangement. The same fruits and vegetables used in a more sophisticated setting – on a rosewood table in a vertical arrangement – show how the same plant material can look quite different (opposite).

Experience in working with fruit and vegetables will enable you to determine the lasting qualities of your specimens. An arrangement intended to last a few days should be made of materials that are in the young stage and just beginning to show colour. If over-ripe fruits or vegetables are used, your arrangement may be going over on the second day, and if you want to eat the items later on, they must be in prime condition to start with. When using fruit and vegetables, a stem must be created which can be placed in the floral foam just as with flowers, and this is best done

with wooden skewers or wooden cocktail sticks, depending on the weight of the item used. Do not use florists' stub wires, as they will damage the fruit or vegetables, which will then be inedible after the arrangement is dismantled. And containers chosen for an arrangement of fruit and vegetables must be in keeping: slices of wood, bas-

To show the ability of fruits and vegetables to look successful in both simple and sophisticated settings, I have used the same vegetables and fruits as in the photograph opposite, in a different arrangement. A base of olive wood sits on the polished rosewood table. A large palm spoon brought back from Kenya echoes the rosewood colouring beautifully. It is supported by a metal stand with a container on the top to take floral foam. Even more height has been created by slender iris foliage leaves, with hosta leaves and nephrolepis fern to the foot of the top arrangement. A small amount only of colourful fruit is used at this height, so that the arrangement will not look top-heavy, and the main weight is in its correct place, towards the base, with the watermelon again used as the chief focal point.

kets, trays and wooden bowls are always suitable. If fruit is to be used in conjunction with flowers, more delicate containers, those of metal or glass, can be considered.

USING BERRIES

Berries – another kind of fruit – have been used by man since time began as food, medicine or decoration, and for me they are one of the major pleasures of nature: they are colourful, interesting in texture and shapes, and can look beautiful in both traditional and modern arrangements and settings. Many can be picked from hedgerows, and of course cost nothing: hips and haws, elder (*sambucus*) and wild privet (*ligustrum*) are all pickable and useable. Many shrubs and trees growing in our gardens also carry berries – berberis, skimmia, pyracantha and the prunus family (see also Chapter Three) – and with the aid of a good plant or gardening book, many more will be found. Berries last a long time in an arrangement, but I do suggest that all the foliage is removed, as it will tend to shrivel if not, and look untidy.

When arranged, berries can look good in most types of containers – in my dear old baskets, for instance, they look magnificent – but to the arranger, containers and accessories made of metal offer stimulating possibilities. If working with a traditional style arrangement, you will depend on reproduction pots, kettles and candlesticks (if you don't happen to have the real thing, that is), and there are also many good modern pieces for those who want a modern setting. I think flower arrangers don't use plant materials in conjunction with their own posses-

sions often enough, and the photograph opposite – of berries and foliage grouped together in a niche, with some of my gleaming copper as accessories – shows how effective such ideas and combinations can be.

Wood, too, is an ideal accompaniment for the flowing lines and colours of berries and, in a slightly grander setting, I have arranged berries in an old oak bible box (opposite). I use this often for large arrangements, both fresh and dried, but I possess several polished wooden boxes which, propped open and containing plant materials, give a Pandora's box effect. As natural as basketry, any container of wood, because of its texture, is well worth having and using. It must be lined, with another container to hold the water-soaked floral foam – a plastic box as in the bible box arrangement, or any container which will fit and serve your purpose.

GRANDER SETTINGS

Just as with simpler arrangements, the flowers, colours, designs and 'feel' of grander arrangements must match and complement their setting. Size is a major constituent of any design. Small arrangements would be lost in many rooms of even slightly larger proportions than the average twentieth-century living room, and I would always prefer – whatever the actual size of the room – that the decorative effect of flowers was confined to one good-sized arrangement than dotted about all over the place.

You can also have fun in what I call 'grander settings' by matching your floral designs to the period of the house, and to the ideas about the use of plant materials that were

Here, berries and metal are the principal features and, grouped together in a stone niche, they look like an old Dutch master still-life. At the back of the niche, a large modern copper tray gives weight and interesting reflections. An old copper kettle standing on a small copper tray is the main metal piece and the container for the plant materials (holding crumpled wire netting). A further accessory, a copper candlestick, gives some balance to the group. The outline sprays are cotoneaster and berberis (thunbergii), used because of their delicate form. The centre of the arrangement needed some definite weight, so I placed some skimmia (japonica) there, both berries and foliage. Sprays of greeny-yellow quince foliage and fruit make a sweeping line through the arrangement (and I have known these fruits to last many months). To give extra weight on the candlestick side of the arrangement, I grouped there a collection of cones – cedar and maritime pine.

In the lower photograph, I have arranged berries in a slightly grander setting, in an oak-panelled hall, so wood – a favourite of mine – is the other principal feature. A low wooden table holds an old bible box which I use often. I like using it with mixed dried plant material – when there is no need for water – but here, with fresh plant material, I have used a plastic refrigerator box which fits the bible box exactly. This holds the soaked floral foam. The shape of the box calls for a natural flowing arrangement – where berry sprays come into their own – and I have used cotoneaster, skimmia (japonica), sorbus (scalaris), viburnum and quince. Ferns were placed to introduce a different shape to the arrangement, and to give weight, a group of maritime pine cones.

I wanted here to echo the theme used by the carver. Long sweeping branches of beech and prunus as well as sprays of sorbus (vilmorinii) create the outlines. Molucella (bells of Ireland) bring in a pale green colouring towards the sides and give height. Alstromeria also flows to the sides. Carnations in various tones of pink, lilac and purple group towards the centre but pride of place goes to a delightful grey-lilac rose called Sterling Silver.

current at that time. Throughout the ages, man has had constantly changing ideas about architecture, art, home decorations, furniture, shapes and forms. Do a little research, look at paintings of the period, at the wonderful carvings on fireplaces, walls, ceilings, mirrors, the decorations on china, fabrics, carpets etc. Flowers and plant materials have always been an inspiration to the craftsmen of the past, and you too can be inspired by their ideas.

In the photograph above, you will see how I have attempted to re-create in my fresh plant materials the carvings on the Georgian fireplace in Warwick Arts, London. It

was a romantic period in which the marble carver created his basket of flowering flowers and foliage, thus the arrangement above reflects this romanticism. The colours are subtle, the shape is strong but gentle, and the setting offered a stimulating possibility for creating something beautiful which would not overshadow the fireplace design itself. Mantelpieces aren't easy to decorate, as the ledges are not normally wide enough to take the size of containers necessary for the width of most arrangements. But here, it was just right for the container I wanted to use – a long, low, white plastic plant drip tray from the local garden centre.

On a drum table in one of the bays in the library at Harewood House, I chose to do an arrangement which would echo the colouring of the books, the gleam of the mahogany bookcases, and the upholstery. I used a large flat bowl that would not detract from the surrounding beauty.

1. Using three blocks of floral foam and plenty of water, I set outline height with sprays of pampas grass and fresh eucalyptus. To the sides, branching forsythia foliage, going a lovely autumnal brown, flows out to create width. In the middle are glossy leaves of bergenia.

2. (far right) To give both weight and depth of colour, I then used dried hydrangea flower heads. Their roundness and subtle colours create textural interest in the group. For how to dry, see page 118.

3. To introduce the main colour, of an orangey-red, and to strengthen the outline as well as the flow, I now introduced sprays of physalis (Cape gooseberries).

4. (far right) With the flowers come colour – glorious peach gerberas, with spray carnations and spray chrysanthemums in tones of copper and peach.

The other main flowers are dahlias and bloom chrysanthemums, used in sweeping lines through the arrangement, bringing colour and form, and completing the picture. You can appreciate from this final photograph why size is necessary in settings of this nature. A smaller arrangement would have been completely lost.

Similarly, if you have pieces of, say, rococo furniture – with both heavy and delicate curves – echo those curves in your arrangements. The containers of this period were much more delicate and elegant than the heavy chests and urns of previous decades, so echo this too in your designs.

And if you have a Victorian setting, take advantage of that as well. Although many people turn up their noses at this period, the Victorians, despite their clutter, had some wonderful ideas. They liked bold, rich and heavy flowers and colours – the variegated, striped carnations, camellias and tulips – and large, full-bodied arrangements were what they aimed for. Their containers too were of all shapes and sizes, many bold and heavy like the flowers themselves. They did have some glorious glass containers though: large trumpet shapes as well as the posy holders and vases (see page 8).

But it is the Georgian period that is my own particular favourite, and I have chosen to do my grandest arrangements in the glorious setting of an eighteenth-century stately home, Harewood House in Yorkshire. The building was begun in 1759, and the house became habitable in 1771. Robert Adam designed the interior, and Chippendale was responsible for many of the furnishings.

The library is one of my favourite rooms in the house. A reception room at first, it was altered in 1845 by Sir Charles Barry to take the overflow of books from the old library. Bringing together Victorian luxury with one of Adam's ceilings, Barry filled two neo-classical bay recesses with mahogany bookcases inlaid with brass, and it was in one of these that

I chose to do the step-by-step arrangement on pages 81 and opposite. Echoing the varying colours of the books, the deep tones of the polished wood, and the upholstery itself, the large arrangement truly looks at home in its setting.

The dining room in Harewood House also displays many of Sir Charles Barry's alterations, but Chippendale's magnificent furniture remains, as well as the wonderful selection of paintings on the walls. In a room of this size, a flower arranger could get overexcited, but I managed to restrict myself to only two arrangements – a typical side-table arrangement, and a grand table centrepiece. The shape of the table in the photograph on page 85 dictated the shape of the arrangement, as did the height of the picture. This arrangement amply demonstrates – along with that on the mantelpiece and others throughout the book – how varied in form, height, width and feel, horizontal facing arrangements can be.

The dining-room-table centrepiece in a magnificent silver candelabra – see next page – is a beautiful foil to the side-table arrangement. Simple candlesticks and candelabra are not easy to work with, but with a little ingenuity and the use of candlecup holders, you can create wonderful effects. Candlecup holders – available in plastic or metals to match your candlesticks or candelabra – are shaped like a scoop, with a protruding piece at the end which fits into the hole where the candle normally sits. Put a ring of plasticine round the protruding piece first, to give a kind of suction that will keep the holder in place, then place a piece of floral foam into the scoop, anchoring it across the top with floral foam

On the dining table, I used the magnificent candelabra given to the sixth Earl of Harewood by King George V as a wedding present in 1922. Although not easy to use as containers – especially this one, with so many candle branches – candelabra do look magnificent. As the 'containers' are so small, only delicately sized flowers can be used. The outline of the arrangement flowing down between the lit candles was made up of variegated ivy and fine sprays of eucalyptus. One or two large ivy leaves were recessed to hide the arrangement's mechanics. Grey-blue freesias and spray carnations in pale pink create the outline, and roses and nerine flowers continue that colour theme. To give the arrangement some further shape and colour, I chose sprays of dendrobium or Singapore orchids.

tape. If using candles as well as flowers, place your candles first on a 'tripod', and then make your arrangement into the floral foam in the usual way. Remember always, though, that the container or containers are small, so more delicate weight plant materials must be used; to reflect the elegance of this particular candelabra, the flowers too ought to be delicate.

I hope that in this, albeit speedy, survey of types of home and styles of arrangement, you have been able to see your home somewhere. If not – and I think I would have to write many more books to cover all the possibilities – I hope I will have at least opened your eyes to lots of ideas, inspired you to try different designs and ingredients and simply given you pleasure.

In the splendid dining room of Harewood House I restrained myself and produced only two arrangements. This one, horizontal because of the position of the picture, rests on a magnificent Chippendale sideboard, fortunately covered with glass, with the added interest of a Chippendale wine-cooler beneath. Sprays of eucalyptus (using both sides for their colour variations), the grey side of Western hemlock (tsuga heterophylla) and grey-blue dried hydrangea heads are the foil for pale pink spray and single bloom carnations. Pink ('Queen Elizabeth') roses carry the same colourings, and cream roses and cream gerberas with pink middles sweep the lighter cream colour through the group.

CHAPTER SIX

SPECIAL ENTERTAINING OCCASIONS

No matter what the occasion might be, flowers somehow manage to contribute that little something special. Whether it's a small informal dinner party, a buffet or barbecue party to celebrate the fourth of July or the fifth of November, or the most formal of wedding receptions, arrangements of plant materials can add to the beauty and the atmosphere of the occasion.

Throughout the year there are numerous festivals that can be celebrated with a party when flowers and accessories can be used beautifully, cunningly and wittily, to counterpoint and emphasise the theme. Christmas is the most obvious celebratory festival, in both religious and lay terms, and because this is *the* highpoint of most flower arrangers' calendars – it certainly is for me – I have given Christmas the next chapter all to itself. But a New Year party could be decorated by an icy arrangement, using glass, white flowers, white foliage to echo the (inevitable) cold outside (see page 111); a St Valentine's party could use the themes of love – the red of those twelve roses and hearts of course; Easter arrangements could utilise all the spring and Easter themes like eggs, little chickens, birds or 'bunnies', budding flowers etc. Summer parties outside can be decorated with flowers – even gardens can be enhanced by floral decorations: see my ideas for a garden wedding reception – and autumn or winter parties, like that of Hallowe'en, which may also be held partially outside (beside a bonfire perhaps because of the nearness of the fifth of November), can benefit from striking themes and arrangements as well.

The floral decorations for your parties can be placed, on the whole, anywhere you like. The obvious place for a dinner-party arrangement is on the dining table, but if the table is small, the arrangement could be elsewhere in the room. For larger parties like cocktail or buffet parties, the possibility of an arrangement being knocked over needs to be taken into account, so its position will need to be plotted carefully. If you're anxious, the room where the party is to take place needn't have an arrangement (a pity, but sometimes unavoidable). Instead you could have a welcome arrangement in the porch, at the front door, *on* the front door, in a front window, in the hall, or garlands twining up the stairs. Even small special arrangements in the loo will tell your guests how much thought you have given to their enjoyment.

As you see, I cannot imagine *any* occasion – or indeed any position in your home – which would not be enhanced by flowers – they

Instead of taking up table space with individual flower arrangements, I decided to explore the idea of suspending wire birdcages from convenient branches, and arrange flowers within them. For the purposes of the photograph, we arranged them beside a table, but do remember not to emulate that too closely, or heads will ache! Flat containers were fixed into the base of the cage to hold soaked floral foam, and the outline foliage line was created by nephrolepis fern and recessed individual leaves of ivy (hedera canariensis). Gysophila ('Bristol Fairy') gives a delicate frothy outline with white spray carnations, pink carnations, bridal pink roses and pink ribbon bows bringing colour into the centre.

can be an icebreaker, for instance, the starting point of a conversation – and so I have chosen a few specific parties from the many throughout the year to illustrate my general points.

COCKTAIL AND BUFFET PARTIES

These informal parties are usually arranged because there are more people you want or need to invite than you can actually sit formally down to dinner. At both cocktail and buffet parties people will, on the whole, be standing up most of the time, so flowers need to be high to be seen. Don't place arrangements on low tables: rather like in church, they will look lovely in your empty room, but will completely disappear when the room is full of people. Keep any arrangements at eye level, place them in taller containers, or in high positions, such as the top of an upright piano or a mantelpiece. They must also be out of the way, otherwise they may be knocked over in the crush. A sturdy home-made ball tree (see page 60) could be set in a corner arranged with foliage, flowers and accessories to suit your party theme – *that's* not easy to knock over! Or you may decide *not* to decorate the party room itself, and simply have a welcome arrangement somewhere else.

Another point to remember about larger parties, and buffet parties in particular, is that plenty of surface 'putting-down' space is needed – for glasses, plates of food, ashtrays, mats to protect your wood – as well as the table itself for the actual presentation of the food. Thus you don't want to take up those potential surfaces with your flower arrangements. In some cases a high stemmed arrangement on a

buffet table might be the best – but only on a buffet table against a wall. If on a central table, around which the guests can move, make sure the arrangement is in a very stable container, or it could be knocked over when guests reach for food. Candles can contribute to a very pleasant atmosphere, and they can be incorporated well into an arrangement, but do be especially sure that they are safe and cannot be touched or knocked over.

As with most parties, try to have a theme – if only a colour scheme – emphasising this with decorations other than floral, with the flower arrangement theme, the colours of the candles, cloths, napkins. The massed effect of such thought and effort from their host or hostess will impress your guests enormously (and might make them sit up and do better when it's *their* turn!).

DINNER PARTIES

Dinner parties are probably the most popular way of entertaining at home, and it is here that the table centrepiece comes into its own. Whether the party is informal or formal, some flowers, however simple, will enhance your table, and make your guests feel welcome and at home. There are certain 'rules', though, that need to be at least nodded at (in flower arranging, many apparent rules are often broken). The centrepiece arrangement or arrangements should in theory be low, thus probably all-round horizontal, so that the guests can see and talk to each other without peering round flowers. This applies especially to smaller dining tables: in the dining room of Harewood House (see page 84), that rule was immediately broken by the height of the candelabra arrangement, some 4 feet (90 cm) high, *under* which the guests were happily able to chat. But this introduces the idea of scale too. Small arrangements on that huge dining table would look silly; height and weight on a smaller table would look equally out of place.

The easiest way of working out the size of an arrangement for a table, is to set the table first as it will be for the party itself. If you place on it the cloth, place mats, napkins, cutlery, glasses, salt and other seasoning containers, you will be able to see at a glance what space is left for your flower arrangement. By sitting down in one of your chairs you will get a rough idea of the height you can allow yourself. Generally speaking, the top of an arrangement in a low container should not be more than about 12 inches (30 cm) high.

The next things to consider are the theme of the party if you have one, the colour scheme, and the type of setting, so that you can plan your flowers. In the photograph on page 90, I have designed an unusual yellow centrepiece arrangement which is more suited to a modern setting, like that glass table top. It takes up a lot of room, but is certainly a talking point, and its bright colours are so cheerful – a good example of the use of colour on colour. I would expect those yellows to be complemented by yellow napkins, and to be echoed somewhere in the design, if any, on the china. I would also expect the cutlery and glasses to be modern in concept to bring about a true feeling of togetherness. On a polished wooden dining table or one covered with a cloth, though, a more traditional dinner service could be complemented by a more traditional arrangement, and again,

a colour from the china design would be picked up by the flowers, and carried through with the cloth and napkin colours.

Once these points are decided upon, the arrangement itself must be considered. Match the shape of your central arrangement to the shape of your table: round on a round table, oblong on an oblong table. A square or rectangular table can take any shape, and if the latter is long, can even take more than one arrangement. But the essence of a table centrepiece is its beauty from all sides and angles, from every place setting at the table; it must also be completed so that its beauty will be apparent at the first view, from above, before each guest is seated. There is really no fundamental difference, though, between a centrepiece design and any other arrangement, because any good design can be adapted for any location, provided you always keep in mind the point of view of each observer. And a final word about flowers on a dinner-party table must be concerning their scent. If special wines are to be served, some wine buff may object to a strong scent ruining the bouquet of the wine. So consider that too, before finalising your arrangements.

I'd like to finish my exploration of dinner parties with a few notes about table cloths. On most formal occasions out of the home, heavy white damask is the norm: a beautiful pure white fabric entirely appropriate for so many formal tables. But I think that we now have the freedom to play around with colour, and the colours of some of today's synthetic fabrics can enhance a table and its setting just as spectacularly. They can be as delicate as you like or as bold as you

The containers here are nothing to do with flower arranging, but office trays bought in a shop sale! Although the top container is the one that takes the arrangement, the other two also hold water, creating reflections and a sense of depth. I fixed wooden skewers with tape to the bamboo struts of the Japanese paper fans. These I pressed into position between the spikes of a pinholder in the top container. Hosta leaves were then arranged in a design to hide the pinholder. Lilies ('Connecticut King') are the flowers that bring that singing yellow into the group.

dare. A particular colour could fire your imagination and create a stunning table. A rich purple, for instance, could pick out a colour from your china, and could be complemented by mixed purples and lilacs in the flower arrangement, as well as lilac napkins.

Fabric *over* fabric could be another idea worth exploring. This is seen par excellence in the photograph of the wedding cake table opposite, but for a dinner party, it could be that white damask or that rich purple cloth covered with lace so that the cloth beneath shows through, its starkness muted by the over-cloth. Play around with ideas, make your own cloths and napkins, tone them together, match them, contrast them, and you will never have a boring dinner table!

WEDDING RECEPTIONS

Ideas for wedding flowers in church were given in Chapter Four, but here I want to give you some more unusual suggestions for the reception itself. An indoor wed-

ding reception in a village hall or hotel would require arrangements fulfilling all the usual 'rules' – following the colour scheme of the wedding, large enough and high enough to be seen easily, placed where they cannot be knocked into or over – and in a house, the same principles apply, but with the arrangements in scale and thus smaller. But I think it's a nice idea to have the reception for a summer wedding in the garden.

The garden itself ought to be prepared first, with overhanging branches pruned back, paths and walkways clear of leaves, lawns mowed. You could add extra colour by planting groups of flowering plants in large containers, and dotting them around the garden. Set up seating in areas where best, but in casual groups, not rows. The tables, too, should be individually placed, rather than one or two long ones. It's informality that will be successful at such garden parties. With no top table – other than, say, a buffet table from which food will be served – the table holding the

For a magnificent garden wedding reception, I chose to make the cake the focal point of the whole thing, situating it under a white-painted wrought-metal gazebo on an extravagantly decorated and beautiful table. The cake itself can be decorated too, here with streamers down the sides (see the next picture for more detail and page 125 for instructions on how to make), and with a small delicate arrangement on the top. Use a small, low, white container to hold the soaked floral foam – the plastic top of an aerosol can will do – and as it is to be seen from all sides, work the whole arrangement at once. Put five side placements in like a five-pointed star, and a central placement for height, and then gradually fill in the arrangement, using that initial placement shape as your guide. Small flowers are vital – lilies of the valley, stephanotis, small dianthus and roses – with small foliages such as tiny leaves of ivy, vinca (periwinkle) and ferns. The streamers are then pushed into the floral foam to fall decoratively down the sides of the cake.

cake can serve as the focal point of the whole occasion, and you can see from the photograph on page 91 how I achieved this. I set up a white painted wrought-metal gazebo, and under it placed a small round table. I covered the table with lengths of cheap but good looking satin fabric, then topped that with a circle of pink scalloped and embroidered lace. This was then over-draped with sweeps of net curtaining fabric (it's very cheap, so you can afford to be generous). Allow a piece of net about three times the diameter of your round table, and pin one end (gathered together with florists' wire) to a position on the less visible edge of the table. Let the material fall naturally into a sweep, as small or as large as you want to make it, and then gather up and wire together with florists' wire. Fasten this wire round a drawing or other pin at the edge of the table top. Swag in this way all round the table and when you reach where you started, cut off the material neatly. I then covered the top of the table and the pins with a circular, scalloped piece of lace. Where you have wired and pinned the swags to the table, emphasise the sweep with satin bows, with long streamers to echo the satin below and pink to bring colour to the table and echo the bridal pink of the flowers in the birdcages (see page 86). The doves just add further charm.

The cake itself, after all that, almost cries out to be plain, and as a flower arranger, I like to have most things, including cakes, pretty plain, so that I have the chance to decorate them in my way! It's a personal thing, of course, but if you like your cake to be highly decorated, with curly edges, pink icing roses, and pillars between the tiers, then you will hardly need any further decoration. I think the topmost arrangement on the smallest tier, with streamers cascading down the sides, makes the whole cake and table setting come together and look rather like a flower arrangement in itself! The streamers are not difficult to make – see page 125 in Chapter Eight, and the photograph opposite – but they must be delicate so that they do not dominate. They should just be part of the finished effect.

As part of the general design of the garden reception the tables should be treated separately, although all adhering to the overall scheme. Although it may not work in every circumstance, I think the hanging birdcage idea particularly attractive – see the photograph on page 86. The flowers and the colouring – as well as the doves – echo those of the focal point of the whole reception, the cake table, and it all looks delightfully peaceful.

Occasionally a marquee may be hired for a wedding reception, and this is always a decorative challenge to the flower arranger. There are two types of marquee – one with internal poles and guy ropes as support, and one that is supported from outside with ropes. Great thought must be given first to the type of reception it is: is it a sit-down meal or a stand-up buffet; is a floor being laid, or will guests be walking on the lawn? Once these major points have been finalised, you will then know what sort of flower arrangements will be suitable.

Marquee poles can be a headache and I am never pleased with them, but various ideas can be worked out. Long garlands of mixed green foliage (see page 57) can be made and spiralled around the poles. Sometimes the guy ropes have to be hidden inside large trumpet-shaped baskets, ideal for flower arrangements: put three or four containers around the pole which will be central inside the trumpet, and then when finished, the arrangements will have an all-round effect. Another idea would be to fix wire hanging baskets at various levels on the poles, with flowers and foliage spilling from one basket to another. Elsewhere in marquees, I prefer to use plastic garden urns to pedestal arrangements, as these have a much more solid base, can't be knocked over, and when finished look very much at home.

The colour of the marquee lining fabric will determine the colouring of the internal flowers, but first of all the wedding colours must determine the lining colours! The marquee is normally put into position a few days beforehand, so you will have time to plan things well. If possible meet the caterers so that you can discuss the flower arrangements with them – there could be some problem that you haven't foreseen. As with most of these occasions, plan well in advance, organising containers, ordering and conditioning flowers and foliage. Give yourself plenty of time to do a good job – it's well worth it!

HALLOWE'EN AND GUY FAWKES PARTIES

Hallowe'en or All Hallows Eve, the last day in October, is the night in pre-Christian Britain when the souls of the dead were thought to revisit their homes. With the themes of ghosts, witches and magicians, you can let your imagination

run riot! Large arrangements incorporating broomsticks, pumpkins – the leering face is by tradition that of a devil – and apples (relating to the Scots Hallowe'en custom of 'dooking' for apples), could provide a wonderful welcome to your Hallowe'en party. You could choose any bright vibrant colours for an arrangement, but orange and black are the most traditional – orange symbolic of the fire used in ancient times to frighten away ghosts, and black hinting of witches, evil, black cats and bats. Masks, witch, cat and bat shapes could be cut from black card and incorporated into an arrangement – or affixed to a nearby wall.

My Hallowe'en arrangement in the photograph on page 94 is wonderfully atmospheric. Be careful though when carving out the pumpkin that you don't cut through the rind – you only want the light to gleam out through the eyes and mouth. (Use the carved out flesh in a delicious pumpkin soup to warm your guests up, or in a pie for pudding.)

Hallowe'en is a festival that is familiar in many parts of the world, but only a few days later there is a peculiarly British festival, Guy Fawkes Night, November the fifth. For most people this day would not

The wedding cake streamers are here shown in more detail to give you an idea of what they should look like when finished. The method is the same as a dried swag (described on page 125 in the chapter on drying and preserving), but do remember to measure first the length needed, from placement in the container at the top, through the flow down to the foot of the cake. You must also keep the size of the flowers and the type of flowers in keeping with the flowers in the cake-top arrangement. Here artificial lily of the valley, stephanotis, roses and blossom were used, with ivy and rose foliage. (These artificial and silk flowers are easily available from your local flower accessory shop.)

For an arrangement to welcome guests to a Hallowe'en party, I chose to feature a grinning pumpkin lit from inside by nightlights which will cast spooky shadows as the evening darkens. On a hessian-covered tin lift on a wooden base in a niche, I first set the pumpkin firmly (a thin slice off the base will help it to stay so), then, in a container at the rear of the pumpkin, I made the arrangement. Sprays of dried physalis (usually known as Cape gooseberries, but also, more appropriately here, as Chinese lanterns) and dried achillia echo the pumpkin colour and give height and flowing width. Chrysanthemums and dahlias and lilies ('Enchantment') are the fresh flowers, and for the strong green foliage needed as contrast, I chose leaves of aspidistra. Fruit and vegetables – tangerines, oranges, apples, grapes and sweetcorn – were arranged (some skewered, some free) to give form, colour and shapes towards the base of the arrangement.

be complete without a bonfire and fireworks, and what better after the outside jollifications, than to invite your guests in for jacket potatoes and 'parkin pigs' (a Yorkshire speciality!) and a good large bowl of hot punch. A flower arrangement could decorate the table where all this is going on, or again be a welcome arrangement, but keep it fun and enjoyable. Use bright colours – reds, oranges and yellows – and introduce home-made fireworks made of dried materials and grasses sprayed with paint; twist together drinking straws with wire so that they fan out into a starburst and again spray with paint. Have these flowing though the arrangement or as mobiles hanging above the table.

CHILDREN'S PARTIES

These are a particular favourite of mine to decorate because sometimes you can forget all about flowers and just go mad. Many people think it's a complete waste of time arranging anything for children except games and food. I completely disagree, and I know a little about it, as I have a daughter and have planned her parties for years. Children love being 'special', love pretty things, and can be a most appreciative and receptive audience.

Take a look at the photograph opposite of a Christmas party for children. There are no flowers here, but I am sure any child would be delighted to set about this lot. The pyramid shape is particularly striking, and children will be excited by its look – and by its contents. The same idea can be adapted for use at any time of the year – eggs at Easter, for instance – but always consider decoration of

some sort for children's parties, even if it's not flowers. Fancy dress parties can have their theme reflected in cake, table and wall decorations as well as costume; some of those Hallowe'en and bonfire night ideas might be particularly successful, but watch children near fireworks or candles. Crackers, paper plates, napkins, sticks of rock, balloons and streamers, all bright, colourful and related, will add to the theme. Going-home presents in gold foil boxes (or in little individual baskets) and some gold-wrapped coins are the sort of thing that I am sure you will enjoy looking out for and I am sure children will love receiving.

This pyramid is based simply on a styrofoam pyramid or cone shape covered in gold foil paper and wedged into a container to give base weight. The decoration is a collection of edible Christmas tree novelties and lollipops: the lollipop sticks acted beautifully as stems; other chocolate shapes covered in foil were pierced with wooden cocktail sticks. These are then clustered on the styrofoam cone, and raided as the children go home!

CHAPTER SEVEN

CHRISTMAS

ith one or two exceptions, I think everyone loves Christmas, and if you *don't* like Christmas, there's really no point in living! Apart from the religious aspects – and the presents, Santa Claus, turkey and Christmas pudding – it's the one time of year when *everyone* decks their homes in fresh or artificial plant materials, with spray snow on windows, loops of cards, garlands of this and that, and, of course, the very traditional Christmas tree. It's also the season when flower arrangers come truly into their own, can create wonderful extravaganzas, can utilise their imaginations to the full – and it's easily *my* favourite time of the year.

Flower arranging at Christmas is no different than at any other time of the year; it's just that the various materials used are different. This is when a riot of colours, glitter, tinsel, baubles – all the artificial, dried and preserved materials – can be used in abundance. Silk flowers, linen and polyester foliages, cheerful artificial lacquered fruits, wicker bells, glass and silk baubles – all these (and more) can be incorporated into wonderful celebratory arrangements. The wired Christmas materials, like polyester vines and ivies, are particularly useful and enjoyable to use: the wire can be shaped in the hands to do whatever you want it to do, but still look natural while giving immense movement to an arrangement.

Another way of achieving colour and glitter is by spray-painting dried and artificial plant materials (I never use fresh in this way). You'll see in many of the photographs in the chapter how effective gold or bronze spray paint is, although I seldom use the silver – it looks more like aluminium. There are many brands of aerosol spray paints on the market, and you will have to experiment to see which you like best. Lay sheets of newspaper on the floor, and place the various items to be sprayed on them. Hold the can about 2 feet (60 cm) away and spray a gentle rain of paint over the items. If the can is held any closer, the paint will cover too thickly and drip off the ends of the material. A second light coating spray will create a much better effect. (Remember to do the reverse of the items if necessary.)

So now, equipped with all your festive glitter, I shall take you through *my* choice of Christmas themes and arrangements, and I hope they will help fire your imagination.

WELCOME RING

This is where the entire Christmas welcome should begin, right at the front door. And it's a welcome ring, *not* a wreath! The ring illustrated opposite was made from a metal ring bound with pine foliage, but you can adapt the idea: a metal coathanger can be bent into a round shape and bound similarly; even a mixed bunch of foliage held together with a bright ribbon bow would welcome as cheerfully! (There are some more ring ideas in the next chapter as well.)

The arrangement part of the ring could be all the way round, but

The front door is where your Christmas welcome should begin, and what better to greet your guests as they ring the bell than this welcome ring. It is made of a metal ring, with pine foliage – lightly sprayed with lacquer to give it a gloss – wired onto it. I decided to concentrate the interest in one group, and taped a piece of styrofoam to the lower arc of the ring. English corn dollies were the first placement, together with cone shapes from Italy and wicker bells from the USA (all with wire stems pushed into the styrofoam). The Christmas colour, red, was then introduced with cheerful shiny apples (of lacquer-covered polystyrene, given a stem with wooden cocktail sticks). To complete the arrangement, I used a bow of red Christmas ribbon (see next page for how to tie).

I chose to concentrate the interest in one group, with some of my favourite basketry and wicker items and luscious red lacquered polystyrene apples (you'll see how useful they are from the other photographs in the chapter). All the materials were given a wire stem so that they could be placed in the styrofoam on the ring, except for the apples, which had wooden cocktail sticks as stems.

Suspend welcome rings on doubled ribbon which is taken over the top of the door and pinned into the thickness of the door at the top. This prevents damage to the front or back face of the door, and it also means that the ring can be swung inside over the top of the door at night if (unseasonal) theft is a possibility.

WELCOME ARRANGEMENT

Once inside the hall, your guests must immediately sense warmth, colour and light – and candlelight must be the most romantic and welcoming. My red candles and red accessories with lots of Christmas greens make a lovely picture, especially with the reflections in the mirror (see opposite). As the candles burn down, they can be replaced with new candles to extend a welcome throughout the entire festive season.

THE CHRISTMAS TREE

The decoration for Christmas, the idea was introduced only fairly recently from Germany, by Queen Victoria's husband, Prince Albert. In those days, they had live candles in little clip holders and blown glass baubles – which you might be lucky enough to find still in antique shops. Modern glass baubles, from eastern Europe and Japan, are just as attractive and they, plus (electric) tree lights, make my tree sparkle on page 100.

I first saw one-colour Christmas trees in California – some about 30 feet (9 metres) high! – and I thought they were stunning. I think red is *the* Christmas colour, so I chose it for my black and white hall (in fact I use red *every* year), but you could have any colours you like or that link in with your room colour scheme. I've seen trees decorated in peacock, lime and turquoise, all toning together. A one- or two-colour scheme needn't be expensive either (although those multi-coloured tree lights might have to go): much of the decoration could be done simply with ribbon bows.

And here is probably the most appropriate place in which to tell you how to tie the perfect bow. Arm yourself with a container or reel of ribbon – whatever fabric, width etc – rather than pre-cut lengths, and with florists' stub wire. The following principle I describe – for a 4-inch (10-cm) bow – is the same whether making large or small bows – just make the loops and tails larger or smaller!

Pinch the ribbon between the forefinger and thumb of one hand 4 inches (10 cm) from the end. Make a loop the same length with the other hand and pinch between the same thumb and forefinger. Keep going with the ribbon across the forefinger and thumb, pinching the same length of ribbon each time you cross the centre, until it looks a little like an aircraft propellor. Make three loops on either side of the finger and thumb, six in all, and cut off surplus ribbon, leaving another 4-inch (10-cm) tail.

Still holding all the ribbon loops in the fingers, take a piece of the wire, and put it across where

I have a great passion for candlelight, and think that candles at Christmas are a must. On my marble-topped hall table I made a candle arrangement, again with Christmas colouring, to act as a welcome into the hall. I taped a piece of floral foam in a heavy container and inserted plastic candleholders to hold the candles very firmly. In these I placed the candles at different levels to create interest. Around them I arranged a complete collar of Christmas foliage – holly, pinus and cupressus. Colour was introduced with wired small wrapped presents, silk baubles, and groups of artificial berries.

The Christmas tree is the ultimate Christmas decoration, and I like to use just one or two colours as a basic theme. Again I've chosen my favourite Christmas red, using ribbon bows, lacquered fruits, wrapped parcels, silk baubles, and tiny lacquered baskets filled with sweets. I've introduced a sparkle with clear, hand-painted glass baubles, with clear glass teardrops on the branch ends, and twinkling lights of one colour. Altogether, as you can see, the candle group, the tree and the presents beneath it (see page 108), create a wonderfully welcoming atmosphere.

you have been holding the ribbon. Push the wire downwards on both sides, trapping the ribbon in the rounded head of a long hairpin shape. Push the petals upwards and twist the wire stems down and together, creating the stem and trapping the loops in the wire. Put a finger into each loop and pull into shape. Use the wire stem to place the bow into an arrangement's foam or to attach to tree branch or whatever.

HANGING CONES

Every Christmas I import hundreds of these cones – pinus *maritimus*, the type you can pick up when on holiday in Italy – and prepare them as in the photograph opposite. They're fairly easy to do, not too expensive, and they look stunning suspended rather like a mobile. They're also quite useful, as they contribute attractive decorative effects without taking up any floor or surface space!

POT-ET-FLEUR

A pot-et-fleur (pot and flower literally) describes an arrangement in a container of growing plants combined with cut flowers (I do something similar in the garden in summer, though with a little artist's licence, I omit the cut flowers). It's a favourite idea of mine, all those mixed plants grouped together, with their different shapes, textures and colours vying with each other as well as helping each other – much better than a long line of regimented pots on a windowsill – and it's an ideal arrangement for any home, but particularly for the flat dweller or those without gardens.

For indoor plants, house or pot plants, can be utilised. In fact, although I haven't specifically men-

tioned it before, foliage leaves can be taken from house plants – in modest quantities only! – like begonia (*rex*), aspidistra, hedera (ivy) and many of the fern family. I wouldn't be without my nephrolepis fern, for instance, for its good looks and its 'cuttability' for foliage: in fact I love it so much I often create a pot-et-fleur of nephrolepis alone, using three or four plants in one bowl to create a wonderful massed effect.

You can use your own house plants, or you can buy a selection from your local garden centre especially for the pot-et-fleur, but in both cases do choose them for their contrasting shapes, and textures: don't buy round plants only or flowering plants only. Have a look at the next photograph to see what

Hanging cones are an original idea of mine. Large pine cones (pinus maritimus) are used, and a length of florists' stub wire is forced between the rows of scales nearest the stem end and halfway round the cone. Bring the wire legs together across the old stem – to make a new one – and twist once. (See also page 125.) A red ribbon bow with two tails and a length of ribbon to make two further tails are then placed across this twist. The wire legs are then twisted together again to trap the ribbons. Make the wire legs into a small loop into which the hanging ribbon can go, and the last action, apart from hanging it up, is to slip a silk candle collar over the top.

I've grouped together for a wonderful effect – something tall, a couple of round shapes, something that trails.

The other thing to consider is the compatability of the plants and whether they will be happy living together. Some may need more light than others, some don't need much water, some are happy with wet feet. As they will be together for a while, albeit impermanently, their combined needs have to be taken into consideration. Choose a large deep container – a bowl from the garden centre, a Victorian washbowl, or an interesting basket (a picnic hamper perhaps) with a plastic liner – and put an inch (2.5 cm) of broken crock in the bottom to help drainage. Remove the plants from their pots, retaining a ball of soil around their roots, and group them together gently until you get the effect you want. Put them into position, using potting compost to fill in the layers and gaps between the plants.

For the cut flowers, I used a plastic cone-shaped container from the florists' sundries shop. The pointed end goes into the soil and doesn't damage any of the roots, and it holds enough water to take the few flowers you'll want to use. Tidy the top soil either with some good green moss or washed pebbles. Be careful not to over-water the plant group, but keep the flower water container topped up. Give the plants a liquid feed occasionally if necessary, and spray them now and then to freshen them (or, in milder weather, put them out in gentle rain).

DRESSER ARRANGEMENT

Many people wonder where on earth they will put arrangements, but all you have to do is clear a deck somewhere. A dresser top is ideal – store those photographs of children and dogs away in a drawer for a rest – and an arrangement like that on page 106 can look really homely with a background of your best or prettiest china. And with a less sophisticated background, you can go again for those favourites of mine, still keeping the Christmas theme – fruit, foliage and candles.

THE DINING TABLE

My dining table, our pride and joy, is always a delight to set up for a party. For the Christmas setting on pages 104–5, I wanted to create a golden or gilded effect – helped by the fact that over the years I've collected so many bits and pieces that I could use, like the brass candlesticks, for instance. I bought one just before we got married, and happily found its mate four years later. The remainder of the effect is achieved by gold artificial Christmas materials – baubles, bead garlands, tinsel sprays, grapes and flowers etc. I particularly liked the gold bead garland effect swinging the whole length of the table. The bead strings come in 9-feet (2.7-metre) lengths, and as it's so inexpensive, you can use it happily and generously to such splendid effect.

To encourage the golden glow even further, gold doyleys were placed under the candlesticks and under the glass side plates. Stiffened cream linen napkins were fan pleated and held together with 'napkin rings' – gold foil ribbon bows. Gold foil boxes hold a present for each guest, and the final linkage is the gold-plated cutlery.

Use the imagination and your own possessions to create a similar effect. Little touches like the doyleys and napkin ring bows are cheap but very effective, and with a

A pot-et-fleur is a container holding a group of growing plants combined with cut flowers. As you see, I've worked in my Christmas reds again, but the height was first created by an ivy plant (hedera canariensis). I then introduced a beautifully spotted dieffenbachia (picta 'Exotica'), and to soften the outlines and act as a focal point, my favourite fern – nephrolepis (cordifolia or sword fern). A plain green ivy (hedera helix) flows over the sides, with a pineapple plant (ananas) lending some variation towards the back of the group. The main flower is the Christmas flower, the poinsettia (euphorbia pulcherrima), and the colour is echoed by a solanum (capsicastrum) or winter cherry, a kalanchoe (blossfeldiana), and a scarlet bow of silk ribbon. In a plastic cone-shaped container (which pushes into the compost in the container without damaging the roots), the cut flowers – five carnations – are introduced. These can be replaced as they 'go over'.

little experimentation, you could have a Christmas dining table that is the envy of your friends!

'FABERGÉ' BOXES

I have always been a magpie collector of everyone else's throw-outs, and there does seem to come a time when some of these bits and pieces make an appearance and find a home. That home could be in a Christmas collage (see the photograph on page 107, and Chapter Eight for how to make), it could be in the 'arrangement' on a Christmas parcel (see page 100 and the following pages), or it could be in what I call my 'Fabergé' boxes.

These boxes, made from 1 lb (450 g) toffee tins covered in fabric, are perfect for rather grand storage – for holding and passing round after-dinner mints, as an earring box, or they could be a very special Christmas box to hold a present: two presents in one! As you'll see from the photograph on page 108, the basics needed are simple. Cover the tin first with fabric – I use furnishing velvet offcuts – but cutting it to fit around the sides and the lid, and glue on carefully. Cover the selvedges with matching or contrasting braid, and the tin is no longer a tin but a background for an arrangement.

Designs can be done in dried, silk or polyester flowers and foliages or, to get the 'Fabergé' effect, beads and glitter: odd earrings, necklaces, brooches, curtain rings, braids and cords. Movement in the design will look best: a dollop of beads in the centre wouldn't look good at all – and scale is an important consideration too. On the boxes in the photograph, the movement was created by wired cord, or by beads threaded onto florists' wire. These are

The central part of my Christmas welcome is my magnificent golden dining table. The central group incorporated a pair of spelter ewers gilded to look like ormolu, set on a polished brass tray. A pair of brass candlesticks were positioned either side, and a pair of reproduction Leeds creamware strawberry baskets on either side of them. The candlestick arrangements were worked first (in tandem as always), after the placement of candlecup holders, styrofoam and candles. Gilded ferns and foliage sprays make up the gracefully flowing outline, and before working on the bauble centres, I attached the gold bead garlands (with strong florists' wire hooks, the wire leg pushing into the styrofoam). I then added the baubles and some delicate tinsel sprays with pearl ends. The central group by the ewers used slightly larger baubles, bunches of lurex grapes and gold lurex flowers. The strawberry baskets carried more candles, foliage, baubles and presents. Altogether, a table that looks as though it's had the Midas touch!

glued onto the top of the lid with tube glue, but if you can't get it to look fine enough, put the glue on a cocktail stick for application. As with a flower arrangement, you need a focal point, so use a beaded earring or an old brooch you wouldn't be seen dead in but which might be the making of your box.

The final stage, apart from the braid, is covering the top with glass. That in the photograph is a domed clock replacement glass. The dome of the glass sits very nicely over the group and means that the tin can be handled without anyone knocking the arrangement off. Clean the glass on the concave inside, and put glue on the outside edge. Drop the glass, glue side down, onto the velvet-covered lid and press home. Clean the top of the glass and finish off with a delicate filigree braid (I look out for the lampshade braid with

The cleared deck of a dresser is an ideal position for a Christmas arrangement, and here I have used my favourite ingredients – fruit, foliage and candles. Using a heavy, flat-bottomed container – because of the weight of the candles – I wedged in styrofoam, and then stretched wire mesh over it to give it more anchorage. The candles (on 'tripods') were the first placement, followed by the sprays of linen ivy and vine foliage. The bromeliad plant below the pineapple looks real, I hope, but in fact is wax. Further fruit colour is brought into the arrangement with made-up sprays of lacquered berries flowing from each side and bringing colour into the centre, where apples and bunches of grapes are positioned. The addition of natural pine cones stops the arrangement looking too artificial.

Collages make
wonderful Christmas
decorations, and I find
them wonderfully
relaxing to do (see
Chapter Eight for
more details). On a
deep gold velvet
backing, I created an
outline of rhythm and
movement with lengths
of wired gold cord (if
you wind it round a
tin or bottle, you get
good firm whirls).
Glued in place, these
were followed in the
main group by the two
halves of a plastic bell
and a lacquered apple.
Trimmed pieces from
velvet leaf sprays give
the foliage backing, as
do filigree gold leaves
and the other artificial
fruits.

These 'Fabergé' boxes are similar to collage work. I cover toffee tins with glued-on fabric. Glue this on carefully, on sides and lid, and cover the selvedges with braid. The 'collage' or 'flower arrangement' is then done on the lid – with anything you have to hand: dried flowers, beads, glitter, odd earrings, rings etc. These are also glued on and then covered with glass to make for a greater permanence.

the fancy edges and use it with the points facing towards the centre). This I glue onto the glass edge and box to cover the edge and make a tidy finished job.

PRESENT WRAPPING

I get enormous pleasure from presents – buying them, receiving them, unwrapping *and* wrapping them. As in the 'Fabergé' boxes, I decorate them wildly with bits and pieces, and, as you'll see from the pile under the Christmas tree on page 100, they're Christmas decorations in themselves. I keep all small and medium boxes through-

out the year from cereals, chocolates, tissues etc, as box shapes are much the easiest to wrap neatly. I always choose a colour scheme such as reds, green and golds: red paper on one parcel, with green ribbon; green paper on another with red ribbon; the gold coming in on the design on the paper, a thread in the ribbon, or gilded flowers, leaves, foil-covered chocolate coins or gold wire. These are all stuck down onto the box in a suitable position with double-sided tape. When I'm really feeling ambitious, I use a little styrofoam into which I make my 'arrangement'.

The Madonna figurine herself suggested this arrangement – the Frozen Madonna – to me. Of very simple lines, she demanded the use of similarly uncluttered material, and I chose first a lovely branch of corkscrew hazel (corylus avellana 'Contorta'). Very lightly gilded so that it would catch the light, I fixed it, by glueing and screwing, on the wooden base behind the figurine. Tiny white sprayed cones and leaves and silver lurex baubles were wired together and fixed to the branches; glass icicles, suspended from the outer branches to catch the light, lead the eye towards the arrangement. The linking silver filigree foliage leaves flow from behind the figure, together with delicate lurex wired tinsel fronds with pearl ends. Weight was brought onto the base with glass baubles, both clear and opaque, and some rather interesting spiky white snowballs.

This arrangement of artificial, dried and preserved materials has a container consisting of two pieces of wood found in a dried-out lake in Kenya. As the wood is so interesting in shape, it wasn't covered up with one huge arrangement; the wood is in fact a major part of the whole design. I wired two pieces of styrofoam onto the wood, and the first placements were flowing sprays of lime-green polyester vines. Once these lines were created, the glycerined (cycus) palms were introduced, as were the budda and lotus pods, to bring the natural wood colours into the arrangement. The slender, variegated fern sprays help to soften the outline, and the clusters of lime-green baubles and grapes bring the centre of the arrangement together. The final placements were the matt brown glass baubles, hand painted with gold motifs.

My 'Cold and Frosty Morning' arrangement is the sort of idea that could be adapted for a New Year party theme, with its sparkling lights reflecting the ice outside. I placed an Irish lustre vase – a family treasure, given me by a friend – on a Victorian clover-leaf-shaped glass cake plate. Into a piece of styrofoam wedged in the top of the vase, I placed large lustre drops taped onto skewers. I made up sprays of delicate silver lurex flowers and used these towards the sides, together with sprays of metallic leaves. From beneath these, covered florists' wires supported the smaller lustre drops. The fruit shapes in the middle are what some people call 'disco' fruit – hand-made in India, and covered all over with little pieces of mirror.

DEREK BRIDGES'
FLOWER ARRANGER'S BIBLE

These gilded angels, in what I call my 'Hark the Herald Angels Sing' arrangement, came, I suspect, from some defunct Italian church. The base is a piece of board covered in plastic gold kid. For the column on which one angel is standing, I used grey plastic plumber's fall pipe – as in the arrangement on page 73. Instead of pasting it and rolling it in sand, I glued half-round wooden beading to the pipe to emulate column corrugations, and then when dry, painted it with black and gold to get the 'antique' effect. Between the column and the lower angel I placed the container holding styrofoam. Gold leaf sprays of five different plant types were used for the outline and the recession. Also recessed are some flock-covered moss-green foliage materials. Sprays of green and gold fruits link in with the larger gold baubles, both shiny and matt.

OTHER CHRISTMAS ARRANGEMENTS

As a flower arranger you will always be wanting to experiment, and to me Christmas is one of those times when new ideas can be created and worked on. People are always asking me what starts an arrangement off, and it's very difficult to give a correct answer. The following four arrangements might give you an idea though. I talked in the first chapter about interesting pieces of wood making ideal containers for flowers and foliage, and in my 'Chocolate and Lime' arrangement on page 110 – which moves slightly away from tradition with a more modern colour scheme – I have used some marvellously curved wood from Kenya and artificial materials. As you can see, the wood is an integral part of the design, its lines suggesting the flow of the dual arrangements. The lines of the vine and fern sprays also show very clearly how good these materials are for the flower arranger: they can be moulded into any shape required, but still have a natural grace and flow. All the individual items like baubles and grapes are given wire stems so that they can be anchored in the styrofoam mechanics of the arrangement. For the baubles, lengths of florists' wire were covered with florists' tape, and one end made into a hook to pass through and grip the ring end of the bauble. (The other end pushes into the foam.) This 'jointing' effect meant the baubles had slight movement, making the arrangement less static.

In the case of the 'Frozen Madonna' (see page 109), it was the figure herself, of course, who suggested the arrangement, calling out to be used with very simple materi-als. The corkscrew hazel branch and the glorious Christmas materials, used subtly and sparely, made a cool and stylish arrangement.

In contrast to this, another arrangement incorporating figurines – 'Hark the Herald Angels Sing' (see opposite) – is much more bold, and shows how the right materials and feel must be chosen in order to use figurines in the best possible way (see also Chapter One). The simple glass and white materials which accompany the Madonna would look quite wrong with the angels, and the gold angel materials would swamp the Madonna. The column in the photograph, like the container on page 73, was made from grey plastic plumbers' fall pipe, again demonstrating how, in the absence of a suitably sized container or Doric column, you can improvise and make your own! Varying gold leaf sprays were used for the arrangement, and recessed were some materials in a green flock. I love this combination, of gold and soft moss green, and the matt flock surface tones down the shine of the gold a little. In all these Christmas arrangements, as you may have noticed, I have deliberately introduced textures – smooth against rough, shiny against dull.

To complete the Christmas section, I did one of my favourites – 'Cold and Frosty Morning' (see page 111) – and it shows *par excellence* the effect that can be achieved by using the beauties of glass – the Irish crystal vase, the glass cake plate base, the lustre drops and the mirrored 'disco' fruit shapes. The silver flowers and foliage emphasise the theme of chill, and with a backdrop art-directed by Jack Frost himself, I think it looks magnificent.

PRESERVED PLANT MATERIALS AND THEIR USES

he preserving of plant materials is not a new thing. For centuries, seed heads and grasses have been gathered for use at festivals and to decorate the home. It was an obsession with the Victorians, for instance, and to this day examples of their work survive in collage pictures. (I make up my own collage pictures, and other Victorian ideas, and you will find instructions in the following chapter.)

One of the principal advantages of working with preserved materials is probably that of economy. Once preserved, the material is always (well, virtually) with you, ready to use when you want. As long as you have storage space, and as long as you store it *properly*, you have the basics for an arrangement – or a collage, a pyramid, a swag or garland – at any time of the year. And many of the items which can be preserved are readily available in the garden (especially if you've followed my advice in Chapter Three on plants to grow for preserving), or can be gathered for nothing from local fields and hedgerows. Another fruitful source, as I've already mentioned is beach- or field-combing when abroad. Many stunning items can be collected, slipped into plastic bags, and brought home. Dried flowers, foliages and exotica from far-off places can also

be bought from florists and flower arrangers' shops. These may be more expensive, but they will last a long time.

One of the *disadvantages* of flower arranging with preserved materials is that many people seem to think an arrangement, once done, should be there to stay. (I've seen arrangements that are worthy of Miss Haversham in *Great Expectations!*) As with any other decorative feature, though, they should only be on temporary display, and should be removed before you tire of them. You can dismantle them after a few weeks, carefully hoarding the individual items to be re-used at a later date. And correct storage, therefore, is vital. I think the best thing to do is to get hold of large cardboard flower boxes and lay the dried and preserved items into them with tissue paper over the top. If they have been used in conjunction with fresh material, allow the ends of the stems to dry before storing. Larger preserved materials, especially branches, can be suspended from a washing line hung in an attic, cellar or garage. A sheet of polythene over the top will keep off the dust, leaving the air to circulate underneath. But *never* put preserved material into plastic bags, as a reaction sets up, and the items can mould away. Remember that they have taken quite a time to collect and preserve, so look after them.

A treasured bronze urn, sitting on top of a mahogany candle stand, holds a collection of finds from many parts of the world. The container needs to be solid for this amount of plant materials, and I wedged a good piece of styrofoam into the container with a covering of wire netting. Starting at the top of the arrangement a good firm line is created by glycerine-preserved foxglove (digitalis) seed heads and bleached stems of molucella (bells of Ireland). Glycerined cycus palm sprays and sprays of mahonia flow down through the arrangement. Glycerined eucalyptus, turned almost black, gives a stark contrast to the cream colourings and the Florida sea grape leaves. Bringing weight, shape and form towards the centre are dried materials – proteas, allium heads, banksia, sprays of beech nuts, and recessed artichokes. For those with beady eyes, yes, there are some polyester flowers in the group – blossom, roses and gerberas.

The following are just a few of the very many plants that can be dried for use in arrangements. Many of the plants will be mentioned in the following pages, but look at the list on page 45 of suggested plants for the flower arranger's garden.

Acrolinium, also known as helipterum, are small daisy-shaped flowers which come in pink and white colours. Cut the flowers for drying before the petals are fully expanded, and hang them upside down in a cool, airy place.

The globe artichoke, that which we eat with delight when the flower is still in bud, can be dried successfully, both in the bud stage and at the flower stage. Cut or buy them as unblemished as possible, and hang for about 4 weeks in a cool, airy place.

Allium, the onion family, are easy to grow and to dry, and they range in size from very small to very large (like this one, giganteum). Hang upside down as usual, but they will retain a little of their onion smell when dried.

PRESERVING PLANT MATERIALS

Many people associate preserving plant material with autumn and winter only, but it can be a year-round interest. There is always some seed head or foliage that will preserve. And using preserved material decoratively is not just for those colder seasons; obviously there is less fresh plant material available, but preserved materials have their own beauty – some natural colour, for instance, and wonderful soft muted colours too – which can be decorative and enjoyed at any time of the year. You'll see a good selection of ideas throughout this chapter. And please don't think of these plant materials as dead. Someone once came into my shop asking for a selection of 'that dead stuff'. 'It may be resting,' I replied, 'but I don't sell anything that is dead.'

GLYCERINE

This is an effective method for branches of foliage and leaves – such as alchemilla (*mollis*), aspidistra, beech, buxus, camellia (it goes dark brown), eucalyptus, choisya, ivy, laurus, molucella (turns a lovely pale cream), oak, and polygonatum. As with all flower-arranging materials, select your sprays, leaves and branches carefully for condition, size, movement, shape etc. Remove any damaged or unwanted shoots, or small pieces (which could be glycerined separately to be used to 'fill in' arrangements or for collages), and then split the base of the stem if woody, so that the glycerine can be taken up more effectively. Choose good, firm, mature plant material, not young floppy leaves, and don't go for autumn colours –

the natural change of colour there means the leaf is no longer supplied with moisture, so the glycerine won't reach it.

You will need a tall-sided container which can hold at least 2 inches (5 cm) of liquid. This is made up of two parts very warm water to one of glycerine. Mix this well, and then stand the cut stems of your material in it. As it is warm, it will be taken up fairly quickly. If topping up is necessary – you must never let the liquid level fall below the end of the stems – do so with the same two to one ratio. Leave the items in the liquid in a cool dark place for anything from three days to six weeks. It is difficult to be more exact, as everything depends on the variety, the maturity, the temperature etc. A rule of thumb is that most plant materials turn from their natural colour to cream to golden browns. Once they have turned colour (and they can continue changing after removing from the liquid), take them out. Never leave them in *too* long, as you will over-glycerine, and in the warmth of your room, the branches in an arrangement can ooze liquid. Hang them upside down for a few days, and the process should be complete. Store in a cool, dry, airy place.

ANTI-FREEZE

Glycerine-based car anti-freezes can also be used to preserve plant materials. Depending on the colour of the anti-freeze – usually pink or blue – pale pink or pale blue effects can be created in the materials.

DRYING

Much the easiest way of preserving, as in most cases all you have to do is pick and hang (see the photograph

Drying is probably the easiest way of preserving seed heads and grasses for future use, because in most cases all you have to do is to pick and hang. A kitchen that is too warm is not ideal – cool and airy is the best medium for successful drying – but as you can see, the drying bunches are wonderful decorations in themselves (and, as you may have gathered by now, I'm all for decorating every room in the house with plant materials, even the kitchen).

above for a well stocked – and decorated – kitchen). The finished items are more brittle, however, than those preserved in glycerine, and must be stored and arranged particularly carefully. You must harvest your flowers, seed heads and leaves for drying at the right time – during dry, settled weather after the dew has disappeared from the plants, and just as the flowers open or when the seed head begins to ripen and turn brown (full blown flowers do not dry well). The drier they are to start with, and the better quality they are, the better they will dry. Take off all extra leaves which will just shrivel anyway.

And start drying immediately if you want as much colour as possible to be preserved. Hang them in small bunches – flowers, leaves and seed heads separately – upside down in a dry airy place (that washing line in cellar, attic or garage again). Leave them hanging in this position with a plastic sheet over them, and choose from here when you want something for an arrangement. If you are going to store them in boxes, you should leave them for about four weeks before packing.

Some plant materials dry better if left in a small amount of water which will eventually evaporate. Molucella is a good example of this. Hydrangea heads, too, can dry well in this way, but can also be stuck into a used piece of floral foam to dry naturally (they'll even dry while in an arrangement). Some people are not too successful with drying hydrangeas, simply because they pick the flower too early in its growing life. The coloured head of the hydrangea is not the flower but a cluster of bracts surrounding tight little ball-shaped centres. *These* are the flowers, and when they have 'gone over', leaving nothing but a small spike, the hydrangea head is then mature and ready for picking. And proteas, when they have started to go at the tips, can be taken out of an arrangement and placed in bottles without water the right way up. I don't hang them because they tend to close up, when they don't look so attractive. Pink or coral when fresh, when dried they turn various shades of cream to brown.

PRESSING

Pressing flowers and leaves, mainly for use in pressed flower pictures, is a popular hobby, and there are many presses available on the mar-

Dried flower arrangements can range from the very simplest – as here, in the Victorian plant-pot holder – to the most elaborate and ambitious. This group of dried pink and white flowers – acroliniums, dyed gypsophila, statice and glixia – can all be bought from flower shops, so they could be the materials used by those who don't have gardens. Having bought, say, two or three bunches of dried flowers in toning colours, separate the bunches carefully (dried flowers are very brittle), and separate the flowers too. Take up individual flowers from each bunch, arranging them together in your hand, so that you end up with a glorious mixed bunch. Tie it round with string or an elastic band, and simply pop into the container.

In a large spelter urn on a marble-topped table, I have arranged larger dried materials, which are mainly available in the garden, or at least locally. They are placed in styrofoam wedged into the urn. To give height I used bulrushes (typha or reedmace), collected from a local pond. Sprays of physalis (Chinese lantern or Cape gooseberry) give colour to the sides of the arrangement, together with delicate sprays of corn (which I bunched together to give more impact). Large poppy heads add weight and a pod shape to the group, for if you're not careful, you can end up with too many spiky stems. Achillea and hydrangea heads help fill the centre, and dried ferns and dried sprays of chilli peppers (no, they're not garden or local plants!) add delicacy of colour and outline. The focal point of the group are the dried artichoke heads and the large pine cones placed at the foot.

ket. I find old telephone books very useful myself, and you can get a great amount of plant material into even the smallest directory. As with drying, only pick your items on a dry day, and you can leave them in the press or book until required – easy storage.

DESICCANTS

Alum, sand, silica gel and borax are all desiccants, which can draw moisture from natural plant materials. Sprinkle some of your chosen desiccant into the bottom of an airtight tin or plastic fridge box, and then place in your first layer of flowers and leaves. Gently sprinkle on more of the granules, shaking the container from time to time so that all the crevices are filled. Proceed with more layers of plant material and desiccant until the box is full. Put the lid on and leave for two weeks. Take the lid off and gently pour the granules away into a tray until the flowers and leaves appear. They will feel dry and papery, and will be brittle, so handle with great care. Store in a clean dry lidded box until needed.

USING PRESERVED PLANT MATERIALS

Obviously preserved materials can be used in exactly the same ways as fresh, with the same types of containers, accessories, ideas, themes, and the same principles – but they can also be used in other decorative ways, many of which I describe and illustrate in the following pages.

ARRANGEMENTS

Many dried flower arrangements can simply be composed of a bunch of flowers literally popped into a container, such as that in the photograph on page 119. Most, however, need mechanics, and the

To demonstrate how useful that plastic bag can be when you are on holiday, this arrangement uses masses of exotic material. The African masks which create the height were bought during a demonstration tour of Kenya. They were difficult to make stable, but I managed to find two suitable metal stands. A large spiked holder was placed between them on a rough-textured hessian base, with a piece of styrofoam on the spikes. Dried banana stems curl up on one side, balanced by glycerined cycus palms and palmetto fronds on the other. Large dried bottle gourds, proteas, banksia, mahogany cones, and dried magnolia leaves help to fill the centre. To stop the arrangement looking too flat, curved giant bean pods come into the arrangement from the left. In a modern setting, with the mirror reflecting a row of cupboards, the fronts of which are made of various stained African woods, the arrangement looks quite at home.

basic is not now floral foam that can be soaked, but dri-foam or styrofoam which must only be used dry. In fact all you have to remember is *not* to wet or soak it! It too can be cut into blocks or shapes, and is a wonderful basis for arrangements. Special pinholders may be needed onto which the styrofoam is fixed (it lacks the weight of water, so is less stable), and you should look at page 10 for instructions on how to fix those. But wedging and taping are also applicable here, as is a foundation merely of modelling clay – used for the arrangement under a Victorian glass dome on page 128.

The photographs on pages 114 and 120 show how more sophisticated arrangements can be built up with preserved materials. Many of them are heavy – especially the seed heads and pods – so good strong containers and mechanics are necessary. Many of the grasses will dry immediately *in* the arrangement, without going through any formal drying process, as will the bulrushes – but those should perhaps be sprayed with matt varnish (the type sold in art shops for spraying charcoal pictures) so that they don't shed their fluffy seeds all over the house. In the group on the candle stand I used mostly glycerined material, but with the addition of some polyester flowers. Many flower arrangers would object to this, but if the colour is right, if they fit in with the natural plant materials, if they look right (and so many of the modern artificial materials do), then I cannot see why not. If you look at the final photograph in this chapter, an arrangement consisting entirely of polyester and silk foliage, fruit and flowers, I think you will agree with me that they can look good!

The photograph on page 121 displays the advantages of taking those plastic collecting bags with you on holiday. The masks of course I bought, but most of the rest of the material was found. Some I played around with to get the shapes I wanted – the bean pods in particular. When bought or found they are very hard and straight. To make them a little more interesting, I soak them in water for a few hours to make them supple, and then wind them into curls round a bottle or tin, holding them in place with string. When dry the new shape will stay indefinitely – but if they sag, just re-wet and re-wind. The same can be done with palm 'spoons', and I once very successfully curled eucalyptus bark that I picked up at the base of a tree in Spain.

COLLAGES

These are a natural extension of arrangements using preserved plant materials. A popular hobby of the Victorians, they are easy to do, and make wonderful pictures to hang or to stand. Apart from plant materials, many other items can be incorporated into collages – shells, cork, beach-combing finds, glitter and beads as in the Christmas collage and 'Fabergé' boxes (see pages 107 and 108).

The prime requisite is a backing board of plywood or hardboard, which can be plain but is usually covered. It can be any shape, but rectangular is the most useful. The backing board could then be set within a frame – a good idea, as it will hide the selvedges if it is covered. To cover the backing board, cut out a suitable piece of fabric – linen or hessian go well with dried materials; velvet with the glitter of Christmas materials –

Collage work is a natural extension of the use of dried materials in arrangements, and you will see in the following step-by-step photographs the principles involved. First assemble, in groups, the materials you want to use.

1. On a piece of hardboard covered in hessian, I first chose the outline material, some side pieces of treated fern. Lay these on the board to give you an idea of the space the group will take up. When happy with these, glue and press them into place.

2. The next step is to go over the same outline design with the next group of plant material, grasses, small seed heads, leaves and more foliage. Glue in place and leave to dry before going on to the next layer.

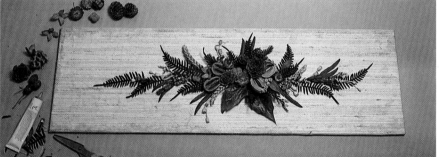

3. And layer is the correct term, for it is not a flat, but a 3-D effect you are aiming for. Different flowers, seed heads, cones and grasses gradually help to fill in the shape. Glue and leave to dry before the next stage.

4. As in any flower arrangement, the collage needs a centre, and here it is supplied with wooden-looking plant material – small proteas, beech nuts, cut poppy heads and beans. Leave to dry and set overnight before hanging. Test first by holding the group up, just to make sure everything is firm.

This collage, too, is slightly more complicated, and although the photographs can't give scale, it is over 3 feet (90 cm) in height. The plant materials therefore are larger and heavier. A thicker type of cane creates a similar outline to that of the other, more delicate collage. Starting from the base, honesty seed pods and skeleton magnolia leaves lead up to magnolia leaves used in reverse so that the matt surface gives another texture. The cream leaves flowing through the group are bleached philodendron leaves, which are a good contrast with the dark linen background and dark plant materials. The focal point is made up of lily pods, gourds, acacia 'flowers' (made up from acacia pods), and the holey lotus pods.

to the size required, about 1 inch (2.5 cm) wider all round the board. Glue the outside edges of the board only, letting it become slightly tacky before placing the material on it. Just as with covered bases, I then stretch the fabric over the board and onto the glued edge. (Again, like bases, if you glue all over the surface, you cannot stretch the fabric as it catches on the glue). Turn selvedges under and glue down, or cut neatly to the edge of the board. This edge can be covered with braid if the finished collage is not going into a frame. If the selvedges are folded over onto the back, cover the back with a

backing paper, or wide parcel tape.

Once the background is ready, you must plan your group, depending on the materials you have to hand. Scale is important – smaller, delicate items for a small collage, and larger for a larger backing board – but so is colour. Just as in any flower arrangement, the first thing to be worked out is the colour scheme. Too many colours together give a 'cheap' effect; you should always go for natural colours with tones of another colour – creams through to browns, browns through to orange, or a cream/ brown basis with a hint of pale pink could be stunning!

As with an arrangement, set the outline foliage first, allowing you to see what space you have to fill with your materials – and I suggest you turn to the step-by-step photographs on page 123 for instructions on how to build up the layers of a collage. This one was simple in concept, but it still shows the basics of collage work – the building up gradually in layers to achieve the 3-D effect, the use of outlines, and a focal point. Each item must be glued on separately: never try to glue on in a group. Always wait until one layer has dried before applying the next, and leave the completed collage overnight at least to completely dry before framing or hanging. Lift it up first to check that all is firm.

The collages illustrated here show more complicated examples of the art, but again emphasising line and movement, focal points – and introducing non-plant materials like butterflies and pipe cleaners! Collages may take time to do, but they can be with you forever. That they gather dust is a major criticism, but a little care with the most delicate of feather dusters can

This collage, done on a tan-coloured backing, is rather more complicated. Just as in the step-by-step collage, the first placements were lengths of twirled cane which gave both the outline and the movement. I wanted to give the impression that the plant materials were 'hanging' on the cane, so I attached seed heads, cones and leaves, with extra movement added by brown pipe cleaners – and why not! A real butterfly hovers to the side of the cane 'branch', adding further interest.

1. *Foliage is essential for a swag, and each piece must be 'hair-pinned' with silver florists' wire. In the back of the leaf, about one-third of the way up, carefully pierce either side of the main vein with the wire, and bring the two legs of the wire to where the natural stem is. Keep one wire straight, and wind the other around it, at the same time catching the natural stem (about three turns should do).*

2. *Giving a pine cone a stem is slightly different. Force a length of wire between the rows of scales nearest the stem end. Take this half-way round the cone, and then bring the wire legs together across the old stem – to make a new one – and twist a couple of times.*

3. *The stems now have to be covered. Take your reel of florists' tape and lay the end of it over the wire just behind the item. Twist the stem to catch the loose end of the tape and squeeze (it's the heat of your hands and the stretching that makes the tape – not adhesive in itself – stick together). Spin the wired leg, holding the tape at a 45° angle, until the tape has covered about two-thirds of the stem. Break off the tape.*

4. *(bottom left) Having chosen your good strong length of spine wire, and wired and taped all its 'ingredients', you can begin to build up the swag, from the narrow foot to the larger top. Pick up the items one at a time, and lay each against the spine wire at an angle. Spin the tape twice around the spine wire and the item wire, which fixed the item – here a cone – to the spine wire.*

The items get larger in size as the swag is built up, and there is also a focal point, just as in an arrangement. On this finished swag – not the one of the step-by-step photographs – it is created by lotus seed pods surrounded by coconut leaves, glycerined camellia leaves and curled aspidistra leaves. These finish off the top and hide the hanging hook.

The welcome ring hanging on the inside of an old pine door is a plastic ring shape filled with styrofoam which gives greater stability. All the items this time are wired – as with dried swags – but the wire stems are not taped; as they're so massed into the ring shape, the mechanics will not be seen. The more variety of plant material, the more interesting the ring will be, and here I have used proteas, cones, poppy heads, beech nuts and clusters of cream glixia flowers.

Welcome rings are not just appropriate at Christmas, but can be made and displayed at any time of year. Here, the ring is used decoratively inside a pine-panelled kitchen. A ring shape of styrofoam can be bought from florists' sundries shops, and it is encrusted in bands with beech nuts and small pine cones. These were glued onto the foam shape. The hessian ribbon bow is ideal for hanging the ring and finishing it off.

prevent this.

Pressed flower pictures can be prepared in the same way, and as they're usually 'squashed' rather than pressed, they can be framed behind glass which is an advantage to those objecting to the dust.

DRIED SWAGS OR GARLANDS

These are the next step on from collages, and can be very decorative indeed. I think they owe their origins to Grinling Gibbons, master carver, who worked for King Charles II and Christopher Wren. His carvings were from nature, and can be seen in many chapels and stately homes. Even if you don't have a stately home, you can still use his ideas as a guide, and decorate your home with swags and garlands!

The most popular shape is long and narrow, as in the finished swag picture on page 125, with a long pointed end at which you begin, and a wider end, the top. Plant materials should be assem-

bled before you start, and must be graded into sizes – smaller for the tail, with larger material for the top – and this applies to everything, leaves, seed heads and flowers.

These are not glued onto a backing board as in the collages, but each individual item is given a wired and taped stem before being assembled (rather like the wedding cake streamers in Chapter Six). Leaves are given a stem as in the photograph on page 125; flowers too have wire stems created because their natural stems are brittle; and pine cones have wire wound half-way round the lowest row of scales before the two legs of wire are twisted together over the old stem (as on page 125 and in the hanging pine cones in Chapter Seven). For smaller work, as here, 22 gauge wire is best. Each wire stem is then taped with florists' tape as in the photograph on page 125; green tape gives a realistic looking stem, but brown is useful too, for it blends in well with natural colours.

This tiered alabaster container is a particular star of my collection, lending a different feel to the 'cone' or 'pyramid' idea. The principles are much the same, the items being larger at the foot, tapering off to the small cone at the top. The wooden base upon which the group sits is an old, round Victorian loo seat (as you see, anything can be used decoratively!). The four graduated collars were made up in the same way as the dried swag, stemmed, then wired onto stub wire; the stub wire was then made into a circle with the ends joined together, and they were slipped onto the various levels. The small crowning cone was made in the usual way, out of styrofoam, and wedged on a pinholder on the top level. The plant materials are dried seed heads, cones, poppy heads and beech nuts with, again preserved by desiccants, roses, ranunculus and paeonia (peony).

Beneath the cylindrical glass dome, I wanted to create a wild flower look. Modelling clay was used on the base of the dome, instead of a container. The flower, foliage and fruit stems were pushed into this, with height to fill the dome and weight towards the base to hide the clay – which sets solid after a while. The plant materials used were all preserved by desiccants, which retain their colour well and allow more delicate items – the daisies and buttercups here – to be dried.

The main features here are a pair of Italian brass ewers, one forming the container. Into a piece of styrofoam, fixed in the top, I placed wired groups of waxed grapes and cherries (salvaged from an old dome display), along with preserved leaves, cones and flowers. A slender branch of silver birch sweeps across the rounded head of the dome, and another towards the ewer on its side, both taking the eye round the dome towards the Victorian stuffed bird resting on the lower fruit group. I've also included butterflies, found in an old family album.

Once the materials are wired and taped, you place them on a good strong spine wire, at an angle, varying the material colourwise as you go – but keeping to scale – and bind on with tape as in the photograph on page 125.

WELCOME RINGS

The photographs on page 126 show how effectively these can be made up with preserved materials, and illustrate how they can be used decoratively throughout the year, not just at Christmas. They could say welcome on the front door, but they could also, as in my two examples, be indoor decorations – why *don't* people use the insides of doors?

VICTORIAN GLASS DOMES

These are ideal for displaying arrangements of preserved plant materials. They are very collectable, usually expensive, but luckily I managed to find a few when the price was right. They hold more traditional type arrangements (see

above) – and you only have to dust the glass! – but you can add little touches like the bird or butterfly, which relates them to their original and most common usage, that of displaying stuffed animals or birds.

The Victorians stuffed their domes so that no breathing space was left – mind you, that's how they decorated their rooms – but for me it's the space that's left that's just as important. As you'll see from the photograph on the left, I also display a collection of antique hat-pins under a dome, and very decorative they look too.

PYRAMIDS OR CONES

For a children's party in Chapter Six, I created a pyramid with lollipops and other sweets, and it is an idea that can be experimented with in many ways. You don't have to be a good flower arranger to do these: the main quality required is neatness in your work.

The basis of a pyramid and of that opposite is a cone shape of

This green, lemon and white cone, prepared to complement the colours of our guest bathroom, is made up of plant materials that have been commercially dried and treated, and which I bought rather than prepared myself. All the items were wired first to give them stems, and then pushed completely into a styrofoam cone shape, wedged into the container, a china urn on a Japanese base. I started inserting at the foot, and worked gradually round, up to the point.

styrofoam. You can buy these ready cut, or cut your own. I once made a cone of about 2½ feet (75 cm) high of nothing but pine cones: I used three large blocks of styrofoam, on top of each other, and carved them to the cone shape I wanted. I then covered the shape with fine wire mesh to hold the pieces together (useful because the mesh can be fixed with wire clips to the edge of the container) and pushed wired gradated cones into it, largest at the bottom, lessening in size to the smallest at the top. (I lived with that pine cone shape for about two years, and then decided it had done its work, so I spray-painted the whole thing gold. With a new lease of life, it lasted a good few months longer, and I'm sure that if I looked up in my storage loft, I would be likely to find it, even now, boxed up for protection and awaiting yet another transformation.)

As you can appreciate, anything can be used in pyramids, as long as the items graduate in size, and as long as they have stems that can be pushed into the styrofoam. Flower arrangers' shop materials often have stems already, other items will need to be wired as in the preceding pages. As you push the items in from the bottom to the top, and around all sides as you work up, keep a variety of materials going all the time – the flowers, the foliage, berries or fruits if using – so that you have as varied a pyramid as possible. You may find on some pyramids that a little in-filling is necessary, and I use dried reindeer moss, available from florists' shops in small bags. Just push small pieces into the cone between the items, and it stays in on its own.

The tiered alabaster container on page 127, with collars building up in size to a small pyramid on the top, is another way in which the pyramid shape can be explored. A similar feel could be obtained by building those old-fashioned glass cake stands up in tiers, graduating from large to small. I keep this pyramid in my sitting room and we haven't tired of it yet.

Running a flower arrangers' shop as we do, my wife and I have seen the development of the most glorious polyester and silk materials, which are a godsend, especially to those who don't have a garden or who can't afford to buy fresh flowers every week. Here, finally, is an arrangement showing just how spectacular these modern materials can be. Sprays of peaches with bloom, black plums, blackberries and grapes, together with wild roses, zinnias, alliums, poppies, foxgloves and fuchsia, are interspersed with grasses, sedges and wild flowers.

CHAPTER NINE

PREPARING FOR SHOWS, EXHIBITIONS AND DEMONSTRATIONS

nce you have got 'into' flower arranging, have developed a style of your own, and have grown to love the art, you may decide that you want to go further, that you want to display your skills to a wider audience. You might start by being involved in a church flower festival (see Chapter Four) or you may want to compete in a show. You may even, like me, want to demonstrate eventually – a profession I'm still enjoying enormously after over twenty years in the flower business. The following general tips may be of help.

FLOWER ARRANGEMENT SHOWS

There is a great amount of pleasure to be derived from entering a flower arrangement show. It makes flower arrangers pull out all the stops to do their best, and helps them gain experience. It is amazing how your flower arranging will improve by entering a competition and, once entered, you will not be able to wait for the next show schedule to arrive through the post.

If you are new to competition, visit as many shows as you can to see what competition flower arranging is all about. What you do as a flower arrangement in your own home is not at all what will be expected on the show bench – which will be larger, showier, and to strict themes and sizes. If you are entering a flower arranging show for the first time, don't, whatever you do, think beyond your capabilities. Think small in the first place, and I don't mean a miniature arrangement either. My first show arrangement was sweet peas and fern in a cut-glass bowl. You must also remain an individual artist, and never change your style just to suit other people. And don't pander to the judge just because you've heard he or she likes pink. If you hate pink, your arrangement will never work.

But the one thing that every competitor must learn at the outset is to be a gracious loser. It's not easy, I know, but you learn in time to take criticism, and that you will lose a lot more than you win. Competing is all about taking part, learning about yourself and your art, and giving pleasure to others. It's nice to win, of course, to find a prize card beside your arrangement, but that's not the whole story. I can remember, years ago,

At the NAFAS festival in Oxford in 1973, I entered a class entitled 'Museum Piece'. I covered a large base in imitation marble paper and placed pieces of alabaster on it at various levels. The arrangement had to be viewed from all sides, so I had to work on it all round. From the top ewer, foliage and fruit flow towards a green drape which carries the eye onto the main arrangement of the group. Lilies, carnations, berries, hops and mixed foliages all flow towards a collection of fruit which again carries the eye on round the base to the next arrangement. It won first prize in its class, but also got Best in Show, the prize in the flower-arranging world, the Julia Clements Trophy. This was the first time the trophy had been won by a man, and it's only happened once since! (Reproduced by permission of The Flower Arranger.)

travelling all the way to Manchester to compete, all of thirty miles but in another county. I chose a class for a green and white arrangement, and went mad spending £5 on a green glass urn, white gladioli, carnations, lilies and a glorious collection of foliage, including leaves cut from my prized aspidistra. Grapes and Granny Smith apples, beautifully polished, completed my arrangement. Never had I seen such beauty, and I thought this is it – Best in Show! On returning the following day after judging, I couldn't believe it, not a mention. Don't know where the judge was looking, I said to myself, but I learned, after a while, that to be gracious is the first rule and to accept that there are people who know better than me!

When entering a show for the first time, send for the schedule and read every word. Not just the class titles, but the rules as to what you can do, and what you can't. Choose a couple of classes to enter: don't think that you can do four of them, that they're easy. Put your talents into just two: one class may take too much emotional effort; in two classes, you can spread it around. Once you have chosen your classes and have been accepted, spend some time thinking and planning. Put ideas down on paper, get some containers together, work with foliage and flowers, and see if your ideas are 'jelling'. Don't think at this stage that your ideas are simple and will not impress the judge. Sometimes it's the *simplest* themes that are most successful. Judges are not swayed by expensive flowers and containers. Never forget that they too are flower arrangers, and they're looking for plant materials that are presented in the best possible way.

Have a practice run at your arrangement if you think this is necessary. Do you need a base, a drape, and if so have you the right one? If not, cover or borrow a base, and if a drape is being used, is it pressed? Everything that is to go into your allotted space must be of the best – an unpressed tatty drape could kill your finished work, and a frayed base with glue showing could lose you a few points. It is the same with backgrounds. The big shows now go to a great amount of trouble and expense using fabric against which you display your arrangement. If you are using a separate background, make sure it is neat and tidy as with the base. I am not a user of painted backgrounds. I know that they are 'in' and have been accepted, but I think in some cases these painted backgrounds dominate the arrangements. Although it wasn't a prize-winner, I think the magic carpet arrangement on page 137, used without any sort of background, tells its story well just through the plant materials and the accessories. When I first started, all you got was white paper covering the trestle table and white corrugated paper curved into niche shapes. This was the allotted area and whatever you did thereafter to interpret the class theme had to be done solely with your plant material without half of the story being told by a painted background.

Once you have read the schedule well, chosen what you want, had a practice run, and staging day is nigh, make sure you have conditioned everything well so that your plant materials will stand well for the length of the show. I have seen flowers and foliage looking very sad on the first evening of a show, which is a shame. Don't forget the public do want to see nice fresh looking arrangements on the last day of the show – they have paid to come in, so don't let them go out disappointed.

When you have progressed through the smaller shows you may be inclined to move on to greater things. I did this also, and I went all the way to London, the big time, and entered my first NAFAS show. NAFAS is the National Association of Flower Arrangement Societies, and they hold an annual flower-arranging festival. These are held at various venues throughout the British Isles now, but then they were always in London, at the RHS Halls in Westminster. I had entered two classes: very ambitious of me, but I thought if I am going to the big city and spending all that money getting there, I'd better make it worth it. In sweltering weather, and motoring down the A1 in my mini van (shows how long ago it was), I had every window open so that the flowers didn't 'pass over' on the journey. When I eventually got to the RHS Halls, I triumphantly carried in my pedestal and buckets of red flowers and green foliage and set to work. If the ground could have opened up and swallowed me, I would have been grateful. My roses had all folded up and the carnations weren't looking too healthy either, and after all that conditioning! The show had to go on, though, and I started the arrangement still lacking roses and focal point flowers. Have a wander around, I thought, and see if anyone has anything left. They had, I begged roses and carnations, and managed to finish the arrangement. Not quite what I planned, but it filled a gap. What joy the following day when I got third prize – and with borrowed and begged flowers!

I treasure that prize card today – my first national prize card – and it just shows what can be done in an emergency. In the photograph on page 130 you can see an arrangement which enjoyed greater success.

If, after a while, you have been doing very well in competitions, you may be asked to do a much larger group on behalf of your flower club. This is where good planning is essential because you are no longer on your own, you are representing your club. As before, read the schedule well in advance and before committing yourself to doing the job make sure you understand exactly what is required of you, and that you are capable of doing the arrangement. In club exhibitions you may be asked to be part of a team, which I personally find rather difficult. Not that I want all the say and all the do, but I wonder sometimes if too many cooks . . . I think the main thing about these larger exhibits is the value of space – not only the space you fill in, but the space you leave – and I think it is a fault often seen at our flower shows: some arrangers just don't know when to stop.

Over the past few years I have attempted many of these arrangements and the Yorkshire Flower Club – the club I have been a member of longest – has asked me to represent them on five occasions. I have been fairly successful for them as I have managed one second and four firsts out of the five attempts.

EXHIBITIONS AND FESTIVALS

Apart from competing in flower shows there are many festivals and exhibitions where the prime purpose is not competition, but flowers arranged by the arrangers for the pleasure and joy of arranging flowers. These shows are either in churches, chapels, cathedrals or stately homes to raise money for the fabric of the building, or to raise money for charity. And a lot of money has been made too.

Many of these are organised by member clubs of the National Association of Flower Arrangement Societies – as indeed are most of the competitions discussed earlier. NAFAS has been going as a national movement for over twenty-five years (although some individual clubs have been in existence longer). It all started many years ago when a group of people who loved flowers got together to exchange ideas. Now there is a flower arranging club in almost every town and village in the country, and about 100,000 people are members of the national movement.

There are also many overseas organisations affiliated to NAFAS,

As a professional flower arranger, I prefer an estate car, because of the flat floor space and the amount of stuff I take to demonstrations. My containers are packed in boxes that can, if necessary, be stacked on top of each other; the bases either lie flat or stand to the sides; and the flowers and foliages are always in water, in buckets inside plastic bin liners.

and I find it delightful when visiting other countries, that I can meet up with people with the same interest: I don't have to speak the language, the flowers do it all for me! The newest development is the formation of WAFA (World Association of Flower Arrangers), and countries from as far afield as New Zealand and Malta are members, all with this common interest – the love of flowers. I have visited many countries, including Kenya, South Africa, Malta, the United States, Belgium, Germany and Cyprus, to name but a few, and I am glad to say, will be visiting many more over the next few years (Cyprus, the West Indies, Spain and Australia this year alone).

So when your club is planning an exhibition or festival, it is a matter of careful thought well in advance. See also Chapter Four which contains a lot of information about planning a church flower festival, applicable here too. When you have been accepted to take part, you will be given an idea of what is wanted and also a date when you can view the situation. Always go along on this 'open day' and get the feeling of the place, and if you are not happy with your siting, do say so. There is no point trying to do your best when you are not happy. Find out if you have to bring your own container or whether you are able to use something already *in situ*. I would always prefer to use my own container and ask for theirs to be removed (if you break or damage it, you may have to organise another festival to pay for it!). Remember also to be clean and tidy, and, as with all flower arrangements, that the plant material being used is of the best quality and condition. Just as with any show where the public will be

In a hall in Surrey for a demonstration to the Cheam Flower Club, I set up my basic bare stage. I like to have three main tables. I cover them with drapes (not tablecloths) which are of a non-creasing fabric, and which reach to the floor – thus hiding all the rubbish behind scenes. I also pretty the main table up with a garland and some floral rings – good to look at before the demonstration even starts.

viewing, they want to see something good. Most flower festivals last about three days, so counting staging day, make sure the plant materials you choose will last the pace.

Another very important point is that the container chosen is large enough to take the planned arrangement, and that space is left for stewards to top up the water level. If it is a special arrangement in a special container, it may be a good idea to explain to the stewards how the arrangement was designed and put together, and the best way of getting at the container for the water topping-up process.

DEMONSTRATIONS

Being a demonstrator is rather a personal thing, and all I can do here is to explain *my* procedure and how, over the years, *I* have managed to work out all that is involved. Obviously I have to plan in advance (just as for any individual arrangement or show) *what* I am going to demonstrate, how many arrangements will fill the allotted time, what principles I shall talk about, the containers needed, the quantity of flowers, the timing in general – and the jokes and stories I will tell! Above all, to be a demon-

strator is to be an entertainer, and it's not something for the faint-hearted. I love every minute of it, but many wouldn't.

So, once asked to demonstrate, having organised timings, venue and all the rest, I pack my car. As you will see from the photograph opposite, an estate car is vital for all that clobber. It's not only the flowers and foliage, it's all the containers as well, and for demonstration purposes, the containers and arrangements obviously have to be *big*! Some clubs I have been to cannot believe that I can get into one vehicle the amount of tackle I have brought, and if there were a prize for packing, I would be well in the running!

My containers are packed into boxes that, if need be, will stack on top of each other, and my bases either lie flat or stand to the sides. My flowers and foliage I always have in water. I don't like the idea of boxing flowers once they have been conditioned, and, in any case,

Half-way through my demonstration, you can see how the lifts on the back tables (they could be milk crates, but mine are those the flower buckets travelled in – I make every item I carry do some work!) have created interesting levels with the completed arrangements. The turn-table is in full swing, and I'm in full flow!

flowers travelling in water are conditioning all the time they are travelling. I use tall-sided flower buckets and plan two arrangements per bucket. If possible these filled buckets are then placed in plastic bin liners which not only keep the flowers upright, but in the summer keep the sun off the blooms (I've been caught like that before, if you remember!). The buckets are then placed in strong grocers' boxes or in those collapsible crates now available. These were originally sold for taking shopping home from the supermarket but are ideal for carrying the flowers (and useful during the demonstration as lifts). I get two buckets per crate.

I always get to the meeting place in good time so that the preparation is not hurried – that can show in the performance. I find out about the stage beforehand – its size, whether it has curtains, whether the spotlights work. If there are no spots, I always ask if it's possible for the club to hire some, for a show isn't a show without lights. In fact, I now carry my own spotlights with me, with an extension cable just in case.

The next thing is the stage. As you'll see in the photographs, I like three main tables – one to work on, and one either side to start the staging for the finished arrangements. In this case there were also some very good cream-painted screens that stood behind the display tables and hid two other preparation tables. The stage must look clean and tidy all the time from the audience's point of view. Now I always look for a rubbish box or plastic bin liners. Once the tables are in position and my preparation area is ready, I then – with some aid – carry in the clobber from the car.

The crates of buckets and flowers are lifted straight out and in, which saves time. I also carry my own set of drapes – which cover the tables – instead of tablecloths, because table sizes vary from hall to hall, and cloths will never fit. You will see from the photograph of the empty stage how, when the tables are covered, all hints of behind-scene rubbish, as well as the various containers and flowers to be used in the demonstration, are hidden.

By the time the demonstration is over, the tables are filled with arrangements – the principles and containers of some of which I'm sure you'll recognise – and everything looks nice and clean and tidy. When the flowers have been raffled and the members have asked their questions, time to pack it all away again!

This being a Christmas demonstration, I added a garland and rings to the main table, which give the audience something to talk about while waiting!

With a plastic sheet over the work table, and the turn-tables at the ready, we can be off. As the demonstration progresses, you can see again from the photographs on pages 135 and 136 that the stage is still tidy half-way through, and when it is over. At the end the raffle for the flowers will be drawn, and before the arrangements are dismantled and the members make their way home, I give time for members to have a closer look at the arrangements and for them to ask further questions. And then, once I've collected together all my equipment, carried it out to the car, said goodbye – it's all that packing up again. All part of the working day of a flower arranging demonstrator!

This is one of the arrangements that stands out in my memory, my magic carpet, which I arranged at the NAFAS festival in Brighton in 1978. It wasn't a prizewinner, but I liked it, and it's been cited many times as a prime example of use of colour. The whirl of carpet was fixed onto stiff buckram and supported by a metal stand which also holds the top arrangement. The plant materials – lilies, roses, alstromeria, buddleia (globosa), croton leaves and curled aspidistra – pick up every colour in the carpet. (Photograph by D. Rendell, reproduced by permission of The Flower Arranger *magazine.)*

GENERAL INDEX

F

facing arrangements 35
fans 24, *72*, *90*
festivals, flower 62–7, *63*, *64*, *67*, 133–5
figurines 26, *27*, *29*, *31*, *109*, *112*, 113
fireworks 95
foam, dri- 10, *122 see also* styrofoam
    floral 9–10, 52, 57, *71*, *76*, *79*, *81*, *86*,
        88, *91*, 99, 122
foliage 7, 18, *33*, 39, 40, 42, 47, 52, *54*,
    57, 58, 62, *76*, *76*, *77*, *81*, 117, *123*,
    124, *124*, *125*, 126, *128*, *130 see also*
    artificial
font arrangements 53, *56*, 57
fruit 11, 60, 74–8, *76*, 94, 97, *100*, *106*,
    128, *129*, *130*
    'disco' *111*
fungus *16*

G

gardens 7, *30*, 39–46, *40*, *41*, 87, *90*
garlands 7, 57–8, 87, 92–3, 115, 126, 137
    bead 102, *104–5*
gazebo *91*, 92
Georgian period 83
Gibbons, Grinling 126
glass *22*, 23, 87, *100*, 106, *108*, *109*, *110*,
    111, 113
    domes 128, *128*
glycerine 117, *118*
grapes, artificial *21*, *104–5*, *110*, 113
green plants *30*, 42–3, 45
grey plants 44, 45
growing plants 7, 39–46, 115
Guy Fawkes 93, 95

H

hand-basin *16*
Hallowe'en 87, 93–5, *94*
Harewood House 69, *81–2*, 83, *84*, *85*, 88
harvest festival *55*, 60
hat-pins 128, *128*
Heptonstall *62*, *64*, 65, *65*, 67, *67*
Hogarth-curve arrangements 35
Holland 23
home decoration 6, 7, 68, 69–78, *70*, *71*,
    72, *73*
    stately 78–86, *79*, *80*, *81*, *82*, *84*, *85*
horizontal arrangements *33*, 35, *83*, *85*
house-plants 101–2, *103*

I

Ikebana 35, 70
Italy 23, *128*

J

Japan 70, *129*

K

Kenya 110, 113
kettles 18, *78*, *79*

L

lifts/plinths 28, *135*
line arrangements 32–3, *37*
Luddenden *55*, 60

M

Madeira 52
magic carpet arrangement *137*
Malta 23
masks, African *121*, 122
mechanics 6, 7, 9, 49, 60–2, 120, 122
miniature arrangements 35
mobiles 95

N

NAFAS 6, *130*, 133, 134, *137*
New Year 87, *111*

O

organisation 52, 62, 65, 67, 136–7
oriental arrangements 70–4

P

paints, spray 11, 18, 95, 97, 129
parties 86, 87–90, 93–5
    buffet 87, 88
    children's 95
    cocktail 87, 88
    dinner 88–90, *90*
    Guy Fawkes 93, 95
    Hallowe'en 87, 93–5, *94*
    New Year's 87, *111*
    St Valentine's 87

PLANT INDEX

A

Acacia 45, *124*
Acanthus 45
Acer 45
Achillea 45, 46, *94, 120*
Acrolinium (Helipterum) 45, 46, *116,
        119*
Agave 45
Agapanthus *38*
Alchemilla (*mollis*) (ladies mantle) *40, 42,*
        45, *58, 59,* 117
Allium 45, 46, *114, 116*
Alstromeria *80, 137*
Amaranthus 45
Ananas (pineapple plants) *19, 103*
Anthriscus (cow parsley) *57*
Anthurium (flamingo flower) *16, 24, 29*
Angelica *42,* 45
Apples 74, 76, *76, 93, 94, 106*
Artemisia, *ludoviciana* (white sage) *44,* 45
        lactiflora (white mugwort) *44*
Artichokes *27,* 45, *67, 114, 116, 120*
Arum (*Italicum* 'Pictum') *24, 37, 42, 43,*
        45
Aspidistras *67, 94,* 101, *117, 125, 137*
Astrantia (*variegata*) *30*

B

Ballota 45
Balm 45
Banana *16, 121*
Banksia *67, 114,* 121
Bay, sweet (laurus *nobilis*) *61*
Bean pods *27, 67, 121, 122, 123*
Beech *54, 57, 64, 66, 73, 80,* 117
        nuts *114, 123, 126, 127*
Begonia (*rex*) *68,* 101
Bells of Ireland *see* Molucella
Berberis 45, *78, 79*
Bergenia (*purpurascens*) *16, 40,* 45, *81*
Birch, silver *32, 37, 128*
Blackberries *60*
Bottlebrush *33*
Bristol fairy *see* Gypsoiphila
Budda pods *110*
Buddleia *40, 137*
Bulrushes *32, 120, 122*
Buttercups (*ranunculus*) *70, 127, 128*
Buxus 45, *62,* 117

C

Camellia *33, 37,* 41, 45, *52, 83,* 117, *125*
Carnations *29, 50–1, 54, 55, 56, 58, 60,*
        61, 64, 68, 72, 80, 81, 83, 84, 85, 86,
        103, 130, 133
Cape gooseberries *see* Physalis
Carrots *75*
Cauliflower *75*
Centaurea 45
Chilli peppers *120*
Chinese lanterns *see* Physalis
Chives *41*
Chrysanthemums *47, 50–1, 54, 56, 58,*
        59, 81, 82, 94
Choisya ternata 45, 117
Coconut *125*
Corn *55, 60, 120*
Cornus *25, 30,* 45
Cortaderia (pampas grass) 45, 46, *81*
Cotoneaster 45, *79*
Cotinus 45
Cow parsley *see* Anthriscus
Croton *13, 137*
Cucumbers 74, *76*
Cupressus 45, *58, 62, 99*
Currant, flowering *see* Ribes
Cytisus 45

D

Daffodils *33, 37, 58*
Dahlias *55, 82, 94*
Daisies *70, 128*
Dandelions *70*
Delphinium 45
Dieffenbachia (*picta* 'Exotica') *103*
Dianthus *91*
Disanthus 45
Dipsacus (teasels) 45, 46
Dock (*Rumex*) *63*

E

Easterledge (*polygonum bistorta*) *63*
Echinops 45
Elaeagnus *33,* 41, *42,* 45
Elder (*sambucus*) *78*
Epimedium 45
Eryngium (sea holly) 45, 46

W

Watermelon 74, *76*, *77*
Weigela 45
Willow *see* Salix
Winter cherry *see* Solanum *capsicastrum*

Y

Yellow plants 45
Yucca 45

Z

Zinnia 45

ACKNOWLEDGEMENTS

I would like to express my thanks to the following for their help and encouragement: the Countess of Harewood; Warwick Arts, London; the Vicars of St Thomas à Beckett, Heptonstall, and St Mary's, Luddenden; Cheam Flower Club and *Flower Arranger* magazine.